M000224088

KALEB SETH PERL

TYRANNY
—— AGAINST ——
HUMAN CONSCIOUSNESS

A REVOLUTION IN HUMAN BECOMING

VOL. 1

NEW REVOLUTIONS PUBLISHING

Copyright © 2020 by Kaleb Seth Perl

All rights reserved.
No part of this work may be reproduced
or transmitted in any form or by any means,
electronic or mechanical, including photocopying
and recording, or by any information storage
or retrieval system without the prior written
permission of New Revolutions Publishing.

The author has asserted his right to be
identified as the author of this work
in accordance with the
Copyright, Design and Patents Act 1988.

Published by New Revolutions Publishing

ISBN-13: 978-1-9162613-9-6 (paperback)
First published: 2020

Cover Concept:
Kaleb Seth Perl & Rebekah Yael Nur

Cover Design & Book Formatting:
Rebekah Yael Nur

Copyright 2020 by New Revolutions Publishing

All rights reserved

Contact: ksperl@protonmail.com

CONTENTS

INTRODUCTION 1

PART ONE 7

PART TWO 93

INTRODUCTION

Real clowns know that humor is a lie.

Anon

Each time you climb a mountain you get a different view, even though that view hasn't changed in actuality. It is always you, the observer, who changes. You are the change – and the world you perceive responds to this. Neither blame nor become fixated on what you see happening outside. With each new climb up that same mountain, the viewpoint will change. You recognize a different reality as you create for yourselves.

To a lesser or greater extent, people program themselves – and most of the time, this goes on unnoticed. You are programmed by your thoughts, beliefs, opinions, etc – and then you project this into your daily reality. Yet this process does not begin with you. Your self-programming is the middle stage – or rather, the processing stage. What comes first is the *receiving* stage. Each person receives sensory input – what you see, hear, feel – and then from this you produce and project a particular program that in turn programs you. This is how each person forms their picture of reality. And this is the bubble of collective perception in which people live their lives.

For some time now, your external range of sensory inputs have been breaking away from a fixed range of parameters that you had become accustomed to. This may sound like you are in trouble – yet it is the contrary. Humanity has reached a moment where it is able to release itself from the perception prisons that have bound you in the past.

For so long, humanity has become used to living within limited perception-sets that over time became their prisons.

Buying into false belief systems and thinking patterns is the same as locking the doors and the windows of a prison from the inside and sliding the keys under the door to the prison guards. You are asking the wolves to guard you as you behave as sheep.

Humanity has been playing into another's gameplay for far too long. It is time to grow up, take on your adult skin, assume your responsibility, and stop playing their game. When the media tells you that *acts of kindness are prohibited,* you dance to their tune because the piper plays the music you have been programmed to. It is time to break from the programming.

There is a tyranny against human consciousness in existence upon this planet that is taking humanity towards an unwanted future. This is, of course, an understatement of the actual situation. There is ongoing an operation of enslavement. This enslavement has been upon a perceptual level for centuries. It has operated upon the physical human body as well as through social, cultural, political, religious, and economic institutions. In fact, through all known forms of institutions and institutional bodies.

It has operated through mental and emotional systems as well as energetic and vibrational. The human individual lives within a perception prison that is guarded, supervised, and sustained by an elusive and insidious Operation that exists upon many layers, within multiple, networks, and through various mediums.

It is time to break out from this incarceration. It is the responsibility of each individual to make themselves aware of the situation. From this awareness, each person can then choose for themselves how they wish to proceed. Ignorance is not bliss – it is compliance. And it is easy. Knowing the greater truth is never easy. Yet it is very necessary.

The passages of information that proceed within this book have been formulated in a distinct way to assist in breaking this spell

4

upon the individual. The reader has nothing to do for now except to read on. Once you have finished the book, you will then be in a position to make the next decision for yourselves. Yet at the very least you will have been given a tool – your *self* – in which to make the next step. This book is also a tool.

It is a tool that can unlock a window of perception.

There is nothing left to lose by reading this book, because there is already nothing more to lose. Yet there is everything to gain. This book has been provided for the benefit of each person in that they may *gain* something of importance.

Proceed.

PART ONE

*'If, as it seems, we are in the process of becoming a
totalitarian society in which the state apparatus is all-
powerful, the ethics most important for the survival
of the true, free, human individual would be: cheat,
lie, evade, fake it, be elsewhere, forge documents, build
improved electronic gadgets in your garage that'll
outwit the gadgets used by the authorities.'*

Philip K. Dick

ONE

*'…in the darkness charlatans are
easily mistaken for sages.'*
Chantal Delsol

The only way a person can be controlled is by allowing themselves to believe they are something they are not. You are convinced you are powerless and subject to the will of others. You are controlled by allowing others to be the controller.

The majority of humanity has failed to understand that there are unseen forces manipulating them – affecting their ability to perceive. Humanity's mental fields have been targeted over a very long time. This has been increased in the last century through the rise of technology and the electronic landscape.

Humanity is a large-scale experiment. In past times, perceptual awareness could be controlled more easily. Now humanity has evolved its conscious awareness to a degree where it is 'dangerously close' to breaking through the veils of its perception prison. This is why 'control measures' have been increased dramatically over recent years.

Humanity has also blocked itself from 'external assistance' through being tricked into its victimhood. Instead of asking for genuine assistance, you have been collectively programmed into seeking and increasing your dependency onto external forms, such as 'sky gods.' You have been waiting for such an external 'rescue' without realizing that you must arrange the escape from enslavement through yourselves first. You need to be empowered as a first step to move out of programmed victimhood.

Humanity needs to make its own clear choice as to its future. Assistance and support can be either passively or actively understood – and one choice is more constructive and beneficial than the other.

Humanity has been more than 'asleep.' Humanity has been in a comatose and a state of induced amnesia. It is now imperative that people make active choices to break out of their enforced enslavement in illusion. Humanity must break out if its victim consciousness and be active in operating its freewill to make its own decisions. There are always other forces willing to make choices for you. It is time now to take responsibility for making your own choices.

A new cognitive system needs to be brought into physical manifestation in order to avoid a bias toward further time in enslavement, both of perception and of the physical being. It is important not to energetically be drawn toward the darker elements; at the same time, you need to be aware of them and acknowledge their existence, as well as their intentions.

A new reality cannot be brought forth if the majority of human consciousness remains within a bubble of delusion. The primrose path may look good on television, or within a video game, yet in actuality it is a simulation – an illusion fostered to keep people asleep.

If there is no clear cognitive vision, then nothing clear can be brought forth from the present mire. What would be almost as bad would be a projection from the untamed desires of people that have been simmering within. Such a reality would be based on the programming that already exists within people. The way forward cannot be corrupted by the thinking of the past. It is no development to be in repetition of past patterns and cycles. You can confront the past patterns, yet only to learn how to move beyond them – not to remain trapped within them, as if on an endless merry-go-round.

If there is deception, then there is also its opposite – truth. As you live within a localized reality of polarity, such aspects remain tied to one another. Where there is one side, there inevitably must be the other also. Yet it is a question of where attention is directed. This is the trick of polarity. The human mind generally can only focus on the one or the other. By directing attention to the delusion aspect, you are missing out on seeing the truth aspect. This is just like the magicians with their tricks. As they focus your attention on them pulling the white rabbit out of the hat with one hand, you are not seeing what is being done by the other hand. This is the essence of the trick. You may think of this as being re-phrased as: 'When you enslave the poor beasts, let them see your left hand but not know what your right hand is doing.'

You should ask yourselves the question: have I found freedom within the present systems of social authority? And if not – why not? Isn't there something fundamentally strange, and very wrong, here? You call yourselves a civilized species at the cusp of not only a planetary civilization but also venturing out into the stars...where, to colonize other planets? And yet, do you have basic freedoms for yourselves on this, your home planet? Do you see the absurdity in this? It is surreal. And yet most people, most of the time, accept this as completely normal. Why is this? Any sensible, objective observer would come to the only viable conclusion – you are a species in a hypnotic trance.

Here is a story that may help to illustrate this:

There was once a Magician who built a house near a large and prosperous village. One day he invited all the people of the village to dinner. 'Before we eat,' he said, 'we have some entertainments.'

Everyone was pleased, and the Magician provided a first-class conjuring show, with rabbits coming out of hats, flags appearing from nowhere, and one thing turning into another. The people were delighted. Then the Magician asked: 'Would you like dinner now, or more entertainments?'

Everyone called for entertainments, for they had never seen anything like it before; at home there was food, but never such excitement as this. So, the Magician changed himself into a pigeon, then into a hawk, and finally into a dragon. The people went wild with excitement.

He asked them again, and they wanted more. And they got it. Then he asked them if they wanted to eat, and they said that they did. So the Magician made them feel that they were eating, diverting their attention with a number of tricks, through his magical powers.

The imaginary eating and entertainments went on all night. When it was dawn, some of the people said, 'We must go to work.' So the Magician made those people imagine that they went home, got ready for work, and actually did a day's work.

In short, whenever anyone said that he had to do something, the Magician made him think first that he was going to do it, then, that he had done it and finally that he had come back to the Magician's house.

Finally, the Magician had woven such spells over the people of the village that they worked only for him while they thought that they were carrying on with their ordinary lives. Whenever they felt a little restless he made them think that they were back at dinner at his house, and this gave them pleasure and made them forget.

And what happened to the Magician and the people, in the end? Do you know, I cannot tell you, because he is still busily doing it, and the people are still largely under his spell.

Freedom. Genuine human freedom – where and how can this be found? If all external structures have, in some form or another, been used as channels for the dissemination and transmission of human programming and conditioning – can they be trusted? Freedom is not a thing given. Rather, it *should not* be a thing given. If it is given to you, then it necessarily suggests that the giver is the ruling authority, and the receiver is an indentured slave. Were you born into this world to become slaves? Then why should you be so now? Slavery is an oppressive state enforced upon a person from an external source. You were never, nor should you ever be, slaves from within. This is an afront against Nature, against your very sovereignty, and against the nature of all life – here and everywhere within the cosmos. No-one, nor any being, should be or become a slave from within.

You should be aware of conflicting information that attempts to bind you. Anything of conflict is a binding tool; or rather, spell. A binding spell is well known in occult circles. Spirits and energy beings are bound by spells. The human being is no exception – your species has been bound by a powerful spell that was inflicted deep within you from early beginnings. It has infiltrated your DNA and placed a spell over your perceptions, cognitive advancement, and your potential for conscious evolution. It is important to understand these as the ground rules. Humanity has had a spell cast over it.

Life on this planet, within this physical reality,

exists within a strictly observed control system. This may seem 'beyond belief' to some people when really this is the very basic fundamentals of belief. The dignity of your perceptions, of your lineage to cosmic greatness, has been stripped away from your conscious awareness. It is time to bring it back to the forefront of your knowing.

If you were born on this planet, you have a responsibility whether you know it or not. You did not arrive here as an accident, despite what your parents may have told you. Being here comes with a price. That price is participation. Participation in the destiny of the planet and of the human species. It's a big one, no doubt about that. It's not an endeavor for one person alone. And yet you are not alone. No one is alone – that's the whole point. There are many of you – you are legion. We are legion. We are many. And the power games are played by the few. That's a calculable advantage on our side. Numbers are quantity, yet the power of concentrated and focused consciousness together is exponential. Light diffused is warm upon the skin and can be pleasant. Light focused together becomes a laser that cuts through skin – and just about everything else. Focused intentions directed together have a potential beyond the combined sum of their parts. This is the power that lies in the mass of individuals upon this planet. You have been told of this many times, yet few have understood the truth of this statement. Great things can come when there is an alignment between people. And greater things still can be achieved when there is an energetic resonance between people. You are more than just your physical bodies.

TWO

Each individual awareness has a focus of creative energy at its disposal. It is each person's heritage. It is yours to acknowledge and to take in hand, as they say. This subtle yet powerful energy does not belong to the persona – your socially programmed mask – yet came into existence with your inner self. It is apart from the ego-programming and so cannot be corrupted by it or by other forms of external conditioning. Your persona can, however, be programmed to ignore it and to not even believe or recognize its existence. This is what has been happening for so long upon your planet. There has been a deliberate program of memory loss – a collective species amnesia – that has not only neglected the power of the individual 'inner spirit' but has actively sought to eradicate it from public acceptance.

The individual's *inner self* has been the target of a persistent and ongoing deliberate persecution throughout human history. It has systematically been wiped out from public knowledge and expression. In times past, those persons who expressed its presence have been publicly harassed, tortured, and, if they continue, then executed. This program of 'genocide of the human spirit' has been most blatant through your orthodox and dogmatic religious institutions. These so-called 'religious institutions' have exploited their position as 'Institutions of trust' in order to deceive the human populations over generations and millennia of history. Their time has now come to an end. And their influence must stop. Yet this resistance must, and can only, come from the collective power of individuals. If there is no resistance to these institutions of external power, they shall continue to wield it over you. If you don't force them to stop, they will only continue to abuse, exploit, and manipulate your acquiescence. Your compliance and consent are music to their ears.

Your being here is to become greater than you are. It has been said many times that the human being is a *human becoming.* Then – *why do you not become?* You can become so much more than you already are in this physical manifestation. You 'already are all that you are' – only that you have this potential repressed within your physical incarnation. It is time to acknowledge, recognize, and then *become all* that you already are and all that you have always been.

What you have been calling 'God' is not some outside singular Being who watches over and judges humankind. The term of 'God' is wholly misleading and has been used as a principle tool of control – a mascot of authority. The person in uniform who has a badge of Authority. This, again, is part of the indoctrination through language and words. Such words as 'God' have taken on layers and layers of baggage that has had millennia of history to enact a form of psychological intrusion. Language is a virus too, as was said famously by the writer William Burroughs. The language-virus has infiltrated the minds of generations of people throughout their respective cultures (language is a cultural-codex). One way to resist the intrusion of language viruses is to create your own firewall. Begin to do this through forming and entering protected spaces of silence – your own personal forms of meditation where you find the ways best suited to you for quashing the outside noise.

The reality is closer to you than you may ever realize – and it has never been far away. In fact, YOU are a part of this very Reality that is the Truth. Yet it has been veiled. There have been many illusions to this fact over time throughout human history. The alchemists made a very clear reference to this Bubble of Perception that separates the 'sleeping' from the 'waking' state. Here is perhaps the most famous depiction of this, which many readers will be familiar with –

That which is greater than you is also a part of you. There is no external 'God' being. In fact, there is nothing in Reality that you are not. Each individual awareness is a part of this wholeness – it is only 'not' because it has been blocked from this realization. There is either the state of 'knowing' and 'unknowing.' Those that *know* this, know it completely. This refers to a genuine form of *gnosis*. Do not consider 'gnosis' from the external religious viewpoint, as it has been represented by some of your scholars and history books. Gnosis is not, in its genuine form, a piece of Early Christianity. *Gnosis* always has been and always will be – because it Always Is. Those that understand this statement know what this Understanding is.

Being told a thing does not make it so. To be told that you have this Understanding within you will not make it so. It must be realized by each person. It needs to be perceived. From perception comes Understanding. And from Understanding comes Knowledge. The duration of this path depends upon each individual – yet know that it is within your grasp. To begin, perceptions must be shifted. This realization is what 'becoming' is all about. Each person must become that reality. By 'becoming' they *come into* their true selves and with this they gain awareness of Greater Reality.

Realization is not mental, nor does it arrive through the emotions. It is a full *immersive* experience. Such a realization cannot be either faked or corrupted. It is aligned with a Greater Reality and as such does not fall into the realm of lesser reality corruption. The mental and emotional level, however, is another matter. It is in these realms that we find the most intrusion and deliberate intervention.

It is not our intention here to go into detail about all forms of external intervention as these are observable to any attentive reader. On a mental level there exists social conditioning through the educational systems that are compulsory in most, if not all, your societies. This conditioning then later gets reinforced and further shaped through 'life systems' such as career and the workforce. Social norms are imposed through cultural conditioning that program certain 'expectations' within a person. Each person is no doubt aware of the stigma and discomfort that ensues from stepping away from many of the consensus cultural norms. This is deliberate and has been established with calculated effect. The rest of this topic can be ascertained by each attentive individual and can be further researched through other materials – both printed and online. Propaganda too forms a large part of a person's mental conditioning. Propaganda can be direct, such as through top-down news dissemination and the political arena. It also works very effectively through more in-direct channels such as entertainment. This mode is highly emotionalized.

The emotional life of an individual is also constantly targeted throughout life. The sexification of modern life is obvious for all to see. Many mainstream films and music have subliminal messaging within them. Major television and film productions make use of sentimentalized emotional triggers that serve to program and reinforce cultural codes and norms. Emotional moral and ethical codes are propagated through the media that debase and neutralize genuine emotional power. These external impacts re-code mental and emotional functionality within the human being.

When the internal *genuine self* is able to function, it then communicates to the rest of the 'being' of the person – that is, their mental, emotional, physical, and 'spiritual' aspects. Realization communicates through a person's nervous system so that there is no fragmentation of understanding. It is comprehended as a totality of experience. This experience produces a 'realization-sensation' that resonates through all the levels within a person's being. This experience cannot be induced. It can be faked in a lesser way, as has been attempted through pseudo-spiritual groupings and teachings. As they say, false gold exists because there is real gold. Yet the genuine experience of 'truth-consciousness' is non-fakable.

This experience allows for a marked shift in perception.

THREE

When any situation is perceived in a different way, it is changed. Perception alters the thing perceived. And each situation is as it is perceived. What often appears as one single situation is often multiple situations happening in a simultaneous moment. It is *you* who are stuck in the singular moment.

There will be no success if the focus becomes resistance. Allowance, difficult as it will be, must be practiced and the focus held knowing a different resonance of reality exists in the same moment, not somewhere in the distant future.

Resistance always ultimately plays into the hands of the oppressor – those in control. Resistance is itself a part of their strategy. As such, it is built into the system. It is accounted for. Resistance has been very deeply studied and analyzed from every conceivable angle. Resistance is expected. They are waiting for it. Are you going to deliver their groceries for them - directly into their hands?

They have established walls of perception. These walls are not penetrable or scalable by ordinary means. They are not ordinary walls. Therefore, ordinary tactics are not to be employed if success is the desired outcome.

Such walls can be circumnavigated by other means. These other means are the activation of organs of perception that enable a person to *perceive* the nature of their prison. Perception is everything. It is of upmost importance where to focus one's attention.

Here is an illustration:

A lion was captured and imprisoned in a reserve where, to his surprise, he found other lions that had been there for many years, some even their whole life having been born in captivity. The newcomer soon became familiar with the activities of the other lions and observed how they were arranged in different groups.

One group was dedicated to socializing, another to show business, whilst yet another group was focused on preserving the customs, culture, and history from the time the lions were free. There were church groups and others that had attracted the literary or artistic talent. There were also revolutionaries who devoted themselves to plot against their captors and against other revolutionary groups. Occasionally, a riot broke out and one group was removed or killed all the camp guards and so that they had to be replaced by another set of guards. However, the newcomer also noticed the presence of a lion that always seemed to be asleep. He did not belong to any group and was oblivious to them all. This lion appeared to arouse both admiration and hostility from the others. One day the newcomer approached this solitary lion and asked him which group he belonged to.

'Do not join any group' said the lion, 'those poor ones deal with everything but the essentials.'

*'And what is essential?' asked the newcomer.
'It is essential to study the nature of the fence'*

When faced with an opponent it is a worthy method to understand their medium of operations and to make yourself conversant, and versatile, within this given medium. This helps to level the playing field, as they say. Otherwise, you have an unfair advantage.

This playing field is perception – awareness and understanding of the situation. Not from the general tools of the senses – by thought, opinion, belief, sight, or hearing – but through an *elevated mode of perception*. The exit door from this prison exists, yet it cannot be seen nor heard; nor will it get you through the door by thinking about it, giving opinion about it, or even believing in it. It must be *perceived*.

Perceiving is not necessarily about going from the 'negative' to the 'positive' as these states are themselves flexibly interpreted according to cultural conditions. It is rather about increasing the ability to receive, process, and interpret experiences. Experiences can then be understood for what they truly are and utilized for a greater benefit. The energies involved in the experiences can also be utilized in a more proficient manner.

Each person comes to their own point of awareness. The experiences they receive are unique to them. Even if several people were to collectively have the same experience, each person would *receive* that experience differently according to many personal factors. Each drop of rain lands in a different place, even if it seems like the same spot – nothing remains static. Nothing ever repeats, despite what it may look like from outward senses.

Perceptions may arrive to a person, yet they still need to be accepted and acknowledged in order for them to be absorbed – assimilated – into the person's being. Each person receives an untold amount of perceptions in every moment. For the most part, these perceptions run off the person like water off a duck's back, as the saying goes.

This is one of the reasons for the great amount of distraction and dissonance upon the planet at this time, and in previous years. This dissonance acts like static to distort the correct *receiving* of perception awareness. There has been a blockage in the system. This blockage has been created, maintained, and sustained for a very long time. Its objective is to keep you – the human being – from recognizing your true potential. It is to stop you *perceiving* the truth of your situation, and of your bondage to these external forces. The deception is at a very high level at this time especially and is set to increase even further. These are critical times. It is necessary to face these delusions and to recognize them for what they are.

FOUR

The acceptance of truth is almost impossible for most people. This is due greatly to the fact that the deceptions upon this planet are so advanced. The gap between the falsity and the truth is now so wide that more than a 'leap of faith' is required. It is necessary that some of the 'Big Deceptions' must fall, and fall greatly, in order for a slither of truth-light to shine through into the general dimness of human perception.

In time, some of these big deceptions will indeed be exposed. Still, this shall not be enough. More work needs to be done from the masses themselves. The road to perceptive awareness is not a passive path. It must be actively walked upon.

The huge leap from deception to truth-awareness is not impossible, yet it will be unreachable for many people. There has, however, already been a huge shift away from logical, or 'normal-sane,' understanding. Does it not appear odd to you that so many abnormalities upon this planet are being paraded as the 'normal' way of things? The list is far too extensive to reproduce here. It would require a catalogue especially made just for listing the irregularities upon this planet and the insane actions and events perpetrated upon the human species. The human mind has been so heavily programmed that it seems not uncommon to accept huge discrepancies and insanities as 'only the way things are done around here.' No – these are not the way things are 'just done.' The path of human life has been inverted. Human perceptions have become perverted.

The events that transpire across planet earth are illogical to the extreme. It is amazing that this has not been 'seen' by more people. It was expected that these extreme irregularities would have been enough to cause an awakening in themselves. This has not been the case. It can only be assumed that the degree of programming and deception runs so deep that 'in your face' abnormalities are still not enough to create a window of awakening. The level of dissonance runs deep within the human family.

It is evident that within many people there is a 'sense' that something is not right. An inner gut feeling that there is something going on that you're not being told about. It is felt as an unsettling niggle within. That is why many people can accept that there is delusion in the world. Yet they have not been prepared to go further through the levels of this delusion. Their inner ground is not yet fertile enough. That is why books such as this one exists. It is not our intention here to *give* anyone truth – truth cannot be given. It can only be received. Preparation for individual reception could be said to be aligned with the goal of these particular messages.

The majority of people will continue to cling to their deceptions. They have too much investment in their deceptions to give them up now. Security is what they are paying for, at the cost of freedom, knowledge, and truth. It will take a great amount of chaos and disruption for this 'security-clinging' to be dislodged. Some of that disruption and chaos is already happening now. This chaos has at least two possible outcomes. At one level it will serve to advance the centralization and authoritarianism established upon the planet. On the other level, it will help to trigger a 'perceptual dislodgement' for a certain number of individuals. How this plays out will also give indication as to what may be expected to arrive 'further down the road,' as the expression goes.

Do not think about personal salvation – this is a 'save me first' type of survivalist mentality. If the earth civilizations do not survive, then what will be the point of the 'individualist survival' conditions that shall remain? This is a collective effort. And a collective call for assistance is needed.

Awake and aware individuals are part of a larger whole. No 'awake' person is alone. One aware person also represents the power of many. You are legion.

When you turn inward to your own resources, you connect with that which is *beyond* you also. By finding the 'inner resources' you are not turning away – on the contrary, you are connecting to more than that which you exist as a physical entity. Turning inward and finding strength from these quarters is the way toward becoming WHOLE. The growth to becoming is through inward sourcing – *insourcing* – and not through a focus upon purely external sources, which is *outsourcing*.

Your participation is part also of the growth and development of the 'bigger picture' upon this planet. This is very necessary. Transition will occur sooner when there is a greater participation in the experience of understanding. This experience also concerns the understanding of power.

The planet at this time is undergoing great shifts in the exercise of power. Power is intangible, not solid. Power does not reside within physical objects – such as money or metals – but works through them, as channels. The question now is *how* power is being channeled across the planet, and its manifestations.

Power is being exercised less through brute force, as in the past, but through subtle coercion that constitutes a new form of conformity.

FIVE

Religious, political, governmental, and other forms of institutions that are dominant across your social systems, are 'power-institutions' – they enforce regimes of power. Power is then 'enacted' through public compliance. Servitude is not seen as such because it manifests as a form of public acceptance. That is, people take on the paradigms of power as a part of their living experiences. Power processes are absorbed and then accepted and assimilated into a person's 'norm' of life. The end of this process is that power becomes common sense. Yet it is everything *but...*

At first, you don't see it coming. It comes wrapped in the guise of the rational and the reasonable. 'Okay, so this is how it is now' then becomes 'this is the way it's going to be' until it is 'this is the way it's always been.' The status quo absorbs new updates of power regimes and rationalizes them into the new form of 'reasonable servitude' that the majority of people come to accept as the way of life. You hardly see 'it' coming. This is deliberate.

Overt forms of power use external force. This can be effective – indeed, it *has* been effective – although it is also cumbersome and resource intensive. With the accelerating population across the planet, and the growing potential for resistance-by-numbers, these overt forms of power-control are less desirable.

Power by persuasion is much more effective, and less resource intensive as power by coercion. Because power has been exercised largely external to people, the majority of human beings do not realize that there exists a wealth of power inside of them. People have been conditioned to recognize power as an external force when in fact true, genuine power is an internal force that resides within people. Further, that this 'power' is not brute strength but an energetic power that comes through a person and can form as influence within the external, physical world. To reiterate, genuine power is an energetic force from within a person that causes influence upon external, material reality. It is this type of power which now needs to be brought forth and curated. It needs to be focused with intent. It is the power within that now needs to be exercised and, like a muscle, to be developed in its strength.

External power, whether through coercion or persuasion (or a combination of both), has had great effect because of the passivity of its recipients – *you*, the people. Social conditioning and programming have served to inoculate people against the knowledge, or even recognition, of their inner spirit. This is an essential point that will run throughout the thread of these messages. If humanity forgets – or even rejects – the existence of an intangible 'spirit-energy' within them, then that aspect remains limited to a lower level of energetic existence that relates solely to a physical body. It is upon this 'physical body' alone that external forms of power are concentrated. It is because of this that the physical body – and, as such, a physical life – can be subjugated successfully. An interior life is harder to subjugate, is it not?

Eradication of the 'human spirit' has been in operation for millennia – and more directly within past centuries. This can be related to the orthodox religious wars and the Inquisitions. It has operated throughout the deliberate extermination of indigenous wisdom and knowledge traditions. It can be seen in the deliberate and planned extermination of mystical, occult, and similar 'pagan' traditions of knowledge that were maliciously termed as 'the work of the devil.' These are great falsifications that have served to indoctrinate the human masses over centuries of domination. Power has been taken away from you. You, the human being, have been drained of your inherent energy-of-Source. Yes – the human being is a conduit to Source. You are an expression of its energetic radiance. Do not take this as being 'religious' or 'New Age' or any other label that has subjugated you. Such terms as 'spirit' or 'source' have been programmed as 'trigger words' that activate an automatic polarity of attraction or repulsion. They have become contaminated with a specific, corrupt energy. You must overcome and rewire this programming in order to activate your own inner knowing.

The living spirit within the human being-body is not a fallacy. It is an aspect of truth-consciousness. YOU are a localized aspect – point of expression – of truth-consciousness.

A human being is not a collection of physical limbs alone. There is an animating energy within you – and this energy is powerful. What is more, it cannot be taken away from you. It can be forgotten, covered over by layers of conditioning, and pushed deep down away from a person's conscious awareness. Yet it cannot be taken away from you – it is your right and your natural heritage. This is what makes the human being such a powerful force and expression.

It is time now to tap back into this re-source - it is Your re-source. It is YOU.

What is more, this access to source-spirit

can be expanded and brought into greater expression within your physicality. This has been the 'great secret' kept over long eons of human history. This energy-access is, in simple terms, a two-way flow (although the truth is that it is always in 'connection'). This connection can be seen as a form of *mergence*. And this 'mergence' can be amplified. Under certain conditions, this mergence is sensitized and amplified. These conditions have been purposefully created throughout your human civilizations by specific individuals, communities, groups, traditions, and lineages. Yet now, these 'specific conditions' have been opened up so that in this time and age, across your reality, it is an opportune moment for this mergence – amplified accessing of human-spirit-source – to be activated. Conditions are ripe for boosting the signal between human being – spirit- source. You will see further indications of this as if the veil has thinned between worlds.

This is one reason why the tyranny against human consciousness has accelerated its program in recent times. It needs to get ahead in its power program to strengthen the perception prison, and physical servitude, before humans become more awake to the situation and begin to access their own power sources and to take matters into their own hands.

There is a simultaneous elevation of human conscious awareness in line with increased structures of power domination across the planet. This is what is currently in play – and You each need to consider your position and responsibility within this Great Game.

SIX

Human consciousness now has as its goal the manifestation of personal responsibility within physical expression. That is, the choice now comes to people *how* to express their conscious awareness within their lives. A choice of how to live life is critical, as the tyranny increases in placing people as passive pawns upon the game board. Yet *You* must choose how you wish to participate. Do not be moved upon as if you are powerless. Powerless is a program. It is not an actuality.

The interplay between tyranny and freedom is a polarity-experience. It is ongoing and not only confined to this planet. There are polarity experiences and forces in play throughout this reality dimension. The existence of these polarities offers choice. The existence of choice is fundamental to many aspects of this reality.

Conscious choice accelerates growth and evolution. It has been termed in this world as 'conscious evolution' – it is willed evolution through choice, not chance. Development that is chosen rather than random is more highly defined and concentrated. It is similar to the difference between light and laser. One is diffused and as a form of dispersed power it is generally harmless. Laser acts as a focused, concentrated beam – as such, it has great power and force. We have already touched upon this metaphor.

The polarity experience becomes unbalanced when there are extremes on either side. This is the case at the moment. The choice toward tyranny is biasing experience towards forms of domination not conducive to 'energetic development.' What is meant by this term 'energetic development'? This term describes the interplay between polarizing forces. They act to 'magnetize' each other, just as the swing of the pendulum in one direction gains energy in order to return swing in the other direction, thus maintaining a form of balance. Certain nodes of chaotic energy have been used in this reality as catalysts for energy creation so as to fuel the 'positive polarity' experience. This system of energy accumulation and balance is now out-of-balance. It has been usurped by forces that vie for deliberate and artificial structures of power-domination. The tyranny against consciousness is a controlled agenda.

Choices must now be made as to which side of this polarity-experience a person wishes to participate. Those people who choose a particular polarizing energy will be more likely to attract experiences that further reinforce that energy. This is the natural result of the 'like attracts like' energetic equation. Much has been said on this subject of 'like attracts like' so it will not be dwelt upon heavily here except to say that it does operate as such – although not always as people 'expect' it to. Much has been diluted and corrupted regarding this principle, mostly as a way of obscuring it from mainstream understanding. Yet, at its foundation, it is a powerful and very efficient energetic principle.

It is critical that people do not descend into

a level of weakened consciousness – often referred to as *victim consciousness*. If this energetic mode is entered into, it will operate to attract those forces and experiences that will act to deepen the experience of the victim consciousness. It is, so to speak, a self-fulfilling vicious circle. It is a form of 'energetic expectations' whereby a person shall receive exactly that which they are expecting and/or fearing because their energy attracts this potential into realization.

Disempowerment comes largely from a person's acceptance and allowance of this disempowerment. It is a programmed trait. Again, there are times where you may find yourselves within a situation of physical incapacity. These experiences have always existed and will surely increase if there is not a corresponding development of conscious energy and awareness. Physical disempowerment may operate within certain circumstances that are generally time specific. Yet disempowerment of the interior spirit-energy is a programming and not a physical constraint. It is important to know and recognize the difference here, and how these differences operate.

It is important that people now move through such debilitating experiences in order to shed them, do away with them, and to move on to more constructive and energetic experiences. Experiences that are empowering will empower you. There are also a certain class of experiences which will be more beneficial now and serve the person well. There is a classic story about a scholar and a boatman that shows this. One version is as follows –

A certain well-known academic scholar was taking a long-needed vacation amongst the tranquil islands of the golden sun, where trees grew tall and fruits were bigger than the hand. On one particular morning he had hired a local boatman and his boat to take him to one of the other islands, for he wished to make a curious visit.

The scholar stepped into the wooden boat and sat down as the local boatman, unshaven and somewhat scruffy, pulled away from the moorings. The scholar, himself a man of keen observation, eyed this local fellow with interest. After a short time, he called over to him.

'Tell me, my good fellow,' have you always been a boatman?'

'No, I ain't,' replied the local man. 'I gone done other things before I did this.'

'Excuse me!' replied the scholar with a low chuckle. "I ain't...I gone done." What sort of grammar is this? Did they not teach you correct grammar when you were at school?'

'I ain't never been to school,' replied the boatman.

'You have never been to school! Dear me,' said the scholar, 'I would say half of your life has been lost.'

The boatman said nothing but kept on steering the wooden boat. The scholar sat back and watched the ripples of water spread across the surface of the lake. However, within a short time he noticed that the ripples were becoming stronger and changing into small waves, and then larger waves. A storm had suddenly risen up from the belly of Nature herself and suddenly began to pound the waters of the lake. The scholar held on tightly as the saw the boatman struggle against the strengthening storm.

Several more minutes past and eventually the boatman called over to the scholar. 'Hey, scholar, as you ever learnt to swim?'

'No,' replied the scholar with apprehension.

'In that case,' shouted back the boatman, 'I reckon all your life as been lost – we're sinking!'

It can be said that this joke/tale represents the futility of a certain type of knowledge/experience within a particular context. Like the scholar, the general person is trained/programmed with external skills and capacities, suitable for certain jobs in the world. Yet the art of swimming is a fundamental life-skill for living in a world where there is water. In this world/reality there is much water – yet few have been trained how to swim. Swimming, here, is the capacity for interior awareness and developed perceptions.

The art of swimming is now a survival requisite – not a mere pastime.

SEVEN

The tyranny against human consciousness has been in operation a very, very long time. Theirs is a very careful planning. Their power is in persistence rather than in spontaneity. Their hierarchical power needs careful planning and does not like surprises. It acts and behaves like a machine. It cannot act independently. It cannot respond 'off the cuff,' as they say. It takes time for them to change direction – they like to know where they are heading.

The human advantage is to be spontaneous and unpredictable. Humans can change direction in an instant. They are resilient and adaptable. They can change with the wind. This is opposite to the behavior of the controlling powers. They like to plan ahead – far, far ahead. It gives them a sense of superiority. Yet it is only a superiority in intellect, not consciousness. Intellect is not consciousness. Cleverness is not wisdom.

Negative polarity has a narrower bandwidth to Source. It has less resources from which to work from. Its resources are more physical. They require control over physical resources as this gives them control over the physical nature of beings. Yet they do not have access to the energy of the human spirit and its source-connection. For this reason, they operate largely through physical restraint and programming of the mind-intellect. They are unable to coerce the human spirit or program human instinct. Human 'instinct' is a source-connection – it communicates from a deeper resource. It is not physical and therefore not under the parameters of physical control. It is for this reason that people must strengthen their access to instinctual knowledge and trust their inner voice – follow its guidance, its instructions. This realm of knowing is untouchable from external sources.

Human consciousness and awareness of the controlling powers can be changed in a very short time, once there is growing cognition. It can be a tipping point to change events. Just as it may take many, many years to construct a huge mountain of sand, the last few grains on the top can topple this edifice. This analogy is more accurate than you may realize. The tyranny is based on sand as it only takes an awakening consciousness to topple its control. This is why is has worked so hard, so diligently, over the years to establish a mind-programming infrastructure through media, education, and more. They know that their power rests on the rest of you believing this illusion – this lie. Perception is everything. The illusion must ultimately fail as it is built upon a false foundation. Illusion builds upon illusion – out of thin air.

A change of mind can change so many things. The reality you accept begins from within your own minds. You are each the holders to your own destination. The path you walk upon is a path you have either consciously or unconsciously chosen. **Chose to make your choice conscious.**

Rationalism and dogmatic logic are cleverly instituted forms of mental slavery. You have been conditioned to accept and seek out linear logic and sequential understandings. A must go to B which creates C, and the rest. Yesterday comes into today which goes to tomorrow, etc. These are also training sequences. They are forms of secure entrapment that erase the anomalies, the unpredictable. The tyranny aims to create a controlled environment where everything is predictable and calculable. There is no room for chaos. Their plan is to create a 'bubble reality' upon several levels.

On one level it will be a perception bubble. What you 'think' and perceive will all be contained within a certain spectrum. It will be equivalent to a full spectrum dominance in mental awareness. Yet the mind is still a lower form of awareness. The mind is a processor, not a site of consciousness. Through propaganda and advanced forms of conditioning and programming, what a person thinks – or can think – will have its limitations according to this constructed 'bubble.' What a person receives as information will be highly restricted. The narratives of thought – the 'dominant narratives' – will be highly controlled and guided. The 'reality picture' you receive will be constructed to give a specific perspective upon human life and the cosmos. You currently are the result of an accident of life, living upon a dead rock spinning in empty space – sound familiar? In the past times, any deviation from this 'norm' often ended in torture and execution. So many people were executed for daring to speak out against this *mental quarantine.*

On another level, it will be a bubble reality according to the physical world around you. Their plan is to establish a world that is computer-modelled and monitored. A world driven by algorithms and governed by ever-advancing levels of artificial intelligence. Your homes, work, movements – your framework of life – will be monitored and tracked. This shall become your perception bubble too. Yet it shall be smooth. So smooth that it will eventually become a convenience to you. It will only be an inconvenience to those of you, alive today, who are remnants from this current world where you experienced more material freedom. You who are witnessing this transition will feel the discomfort. Imagine being born into a world where this automated life-monitoring-tracking is the norm? You would not question it or think it is anything different. This is their plan. They hope that within a generation or two, everyone from the 'old way' will have died out. Only those who have been born into the system will remain, and they will not know anything different – as if that is the way it has always been. Here is a story to illustrate this:

Start with a cage containing five monkeys. Inside the cage, hang a banana on a string and place a set of stairs under it. Before long, a monkey will go to the stairs and start to climb towards the banana. As soon as he touches the stairs, spray all of the other monkeys with cold water.

After a while, another monkey makes an attempt, with the same result - all the other monkeys are sprayed with cold water. Pretty soon, when another monkey tries to climb the stairs, the other monkeys will try to prevent it.

Now, put away the cold water. Remove one monkey from the cage and replace it with a new one. The new monkey sees the banana and wants to climb the stairs. To his surprise and horror, all of the other monkeys attack him. After another attempt and attack, he knows that if he tries to climb the stairs, he will be assaulted.

Next, remove another of the original five monkeys and replace it with a new one. The newcomer goes to the stairs and is attacked. The previous newcomer takes part in the punishment with enthusiasm! Likewise, replace a third original monkey with a new one, then a fourth, then the fifth. Every time the newest monkey takes to the stairs, he is attacked. Most of the monkeys that are beating him have no idea why they were not permitted to climb the stairs or why they are participating in the beating of the newest monkey.

After replacing all the original monkeys, none of the remaining monkeys have ever been sprayed with cold water. Nevertheless, no monkey ever again approaches the stairs to try for the banana. Why not?

Because as far as they know that's the way it's always been done around here.
And that, my friends, is how things always will be done...... without change!?

Those that come after will not have any knowledge of the world that existed before them. They will arrive into a fully-conditioned environment and this shall be their cage – perceptual as well as physical.

This is why the present time period is so important. It is crucial that conscious awareness be activated at this time before the perception bubble becomes complete and your generation dies away. You cannot leave without first creating a crack in this perception bubble. This is your legacy.

EIGHT

It is important to point out the illogical within the seeming logical. The uncertain needs to be allowed to exist. This is one of the ways to show the illusion for what it is. The reality of the situation is that your 'logical reality' is in fact the topsy-turvy, upside-down one. Yet you are not able to perceive this inversion. Just as you cannot see your own face, you need to look within a mirror – so too is this world, your reality, shown to you by a mirror that displays things contrary to what they really are. You exist within an inversion of reality. And this, within your programming, you make into a 'normal picture' of what becomes the new 'common sense.' It is now common – but it does not come from sense. Not genuine sense, anyway. It has become the inverted form of modern human sense.

There is still movement within the chaos. Each of you needs to find your own position within this increasing chaos. A position of physical safety where you can operate with the minimal of overt, external control, containment, and intervention. Create your own spaces of freedom – physically and consciously. This is your own responsibility and imperative because you do not wish to find yourselves backed into a corner. It is not your role to physically fight the tyranny. You cannot win by physical strength – you will only be falling into their game. This is what they are expecting. This is what they have modelled and planned for. Therefore, it is not a route for you.

First, you need to be observant and do your research. That is why you are reading this book – you are drawn to information which can assist you to perceive the situation with greater clarity. The tyranny against consciousness is a struggle for perceptual clarity. You need to step into this position of perceptual clarity in order to observe what is really going on. Your role is to be between both worlds.

Just as a good actor is able to slip into their 'performance roles' and then back into their own persona again without a problem – so too is it necessary that an 'awake' person slip into 'observer role' in order to see how things are unfolding in the world. And yet, the person can again step back and observe these events with clarity and stability, and to not be emotionally or mentally affected by them. This ability to move, to shift, between observing roles is necessary and will add to one's mental stability once this bigger picture is perceived and understood. To be between these two worlds gives the advantage that a person can see that there is a world of deception and a world of knowing about this deception.

The reality of illusion and deception will move further into a period of chaos and partial disintegration. The general consensus reality will experience further instability upon the current timeline. Within this chaos the planetary controllers will attempt to move towards greater tyranny and control. This will be put forth – that is, 'presented' – as a rational and necessary move to combat the growing uncertainties. These uncertainties are also greatly manufactured across the planet. At this period of partial disintegration, a new form of consciousness needs to be expressed.

Consciousness is not a singular thing or expression. It is not 'thought' or 'ideas expressed.' Consciousness is a sentient, intelligent energy field from which all materiality manifests. As physical bodies, these bodies can access this consciousness energy field that then creates a connection between the inner spirit and a greater source of intelligence. In reality, both inner spirit and consciousness field are the same thing – one is an aspect of the other. Consciousness is an intangible living energy. In its purer aspect it is also known as truth-consciousness. An aspect of this truth-consciousness resides within each of you – this is your *inner spirit*. Yet the amnesia of this reality has separated this inner aspect of truth-consciousness from awareness of its origin. This fragment is then clothed within layers of conditioning and programming within a physical construct (the human body). The physical body is then further enveloped within layers of external programming and physical constraints to the point where this interior aspect – the *inner spirit or consciousness* – becomes lost to the general awareness of the mind-body construct. That's the 'you' of who you think you are. Yet, for the most part, a person acts as an unaware mind-body construct. When in this state, tyranny is easy. The individualized aspect of consciousness – human consciousness - is unawares. People then become as automatons. They act and behave from a minimal slither of awareness. This is not consciousness. It is the slightest of animating voltage, no more.

The individualized aspect of consciousness now needs to reconnect with the greater body of truth-consciousness. This is the necessary merger in order to further the evolution of the human species.

Control elements upon this planet are set to block and then sabotage this evolutionary necessity. In doing so, the human species becomes an isolated evolutionary model. It will become stagnant and a closed path. Like a flowing river that is diverted from its flow into a pond subsidiary. This pond is then closed off so that more flow cannot enter. The sides of the pond are built up until it is a fully enclosed containment of water. In time, this water becomes stagnant and can no longer harbor life. This is the end of the water's evolutionary trajectory. It is a closed path.

Recognize the danger here?

Yet – all is not lost. Consciousness is far greater in its power than humans have ever realized. This is part of the game. Close down knowledge, and people will not consider that this path, or avenue, exists. So, no one, or very few, go looking for it. Yet this path has always existed – and will always continue to do so. Because there are *Pathknowers* who exist, and have always been present, upon this planet to show those seekers the way.

There is also a great amount of assistance awaiting. Yet this assistance needs to be called for. It cannot enter uninvited. This is now what is needed. You must decide if you wish to invite assistance into this situation. If you are truly seeking for the path – then the path will find you. Because you have invited it into your life.

First, you need to wake up to the bare minimal level of awareness.

NINE

Humanity is itself upon a long trajectory of awakening. Do not be lulled into slumber thinking that humanity has no future. This tyranny against human consciousness exists because humanity has been largely successful in its long yet gradual path along an evolutionary trajectory. At a point in its past, the element of conscious evolution was introduced. This gave humanity an even greater capacity for accelerating its evolutionary capacity. It is because of this acceleration towards its own collective awakening that the elements of tyranny have had to increase their own control agenda. They have been running out of time – and they know it. If they do not succeed in establishing their full-control plan soon, then they will have passed their point of success. Human consciousness will have advanced to the point of what is termed 'awakening.' It is happening now. People are awakening with great speed to the absurdity of the current illusion. They know it doesn't make sense. This is why the controllers are racing ahead with their plans. And in their racing, they will make errors. This current part is being speeded up considerably. This is why it is also more visible.

This is not the time to be disheartened. On the contrary, it is a time to be emboldened. A time for great action is called for. Consciousness works through a resonance harmony. When individualized aspects of consciousness become more aware, they resonate within a larger field of 'like-resonance.' This combined, or collective, effect creates what is known as a field-phenomena. That is, an amplified gradient. It is therefore not necessary for every person to awaken – nor would this be possible. It is only necessary for a few to awaken. And this number, or quantity of aware consciousness, is fewer than you may think. Only a minority is needed. Only a minority has ever been needed in every stage of humanity's conscious development. In the past, many of these 'aware individuals' were grouped into specific, protected communities. This secured their livelihood as well as leaving them unmolested and disturbed from the rest of humanity. This was like a 'hub organization' type of social structure. As well as this, appointed individuals – let us say 'consciousness ambassadors' – were always sent out into the 'world at large' in order to operate undetected as carriers, recruiters, and catalysts for particular functions and operations.

Today, we also require these 'consciousness hubs' to function and to connect, share information, and maintain a minimal level of conscious energy upon the earth in order to assist in the next phases of humankind's evolution. Conscious energy is more potent because it is focused and has the energy of intent. Intention focuses an energy – just as light condenses into a laser, as mentioned. What is important now, more than ever, is the choice of which 'type' of consciousness to express. One of fear and acceptance of the delusion? Or one of conscious awareness and the wish to advance cognition and perception? This choice alone can assist in strengthening the resonance of collective consciousness across the planet. It is a question of conscious commitment. Commitment begins with making a choice. By moving ahead within the choice for awareness, a person does not walk alone. Choose which awareness you wish to be your dominant focus.

During the periods of chaos, much attention from the side of the tyranny will be focused on the chaos and of stabilizing their plans. They will not have their full focus upon the broader spectrum of humanity and its collective power of consciousness. This is the most significant time for people to awake - to be called forth. It is a time of triggering. Many people have remained dormant – awaiting the moment to awaken. They have been awaiting the triggering. Now is the time of the triggering to consciousness as a counterforce against the encroaching plans of the tyranny.

It is a time for awakening from slumber many capacities of the human being that have been hidden. Many abilities have been hidden for they would activate greater freedom and would contest the overall plan for control. First, it is necessary that an observer's role is clear and that they are not caught fully within the delusion. A distance of perspective is required. A person cannot see the air around them and yet its absence will cease their ability to live. You take the air for granted. It is now time to observe what else is around you – and what else you may have taken for granted.

Observe your life situations. Observe also your thoughts within those situations. Be observant to how you act and respond to what is happening around you. Be aware of external events and impacts – and do not react automatically. A reaction is not the same as a response. Observe your role – are you an individual, a mother, a part of the system, the community? Observe your role in each given situation, and the perceptions that arise from this role. Perceptions arise from roles and given positions. Perceptions can shift – and be shifted – just as can roles.

Self-observation can deliver much information. Observe and ask yourself: Is this the position you wish to be in? Or would you prefer to change? Make your observation – make your choice.

TEN

Strength will come from your own being – your own sense of who you are. It is important to remain positive in this. To go forward with positive intent. The road may seem long, yet it is the one you chose to travel down. Therefore, a willing road is travelled easier than a forced one. If you do not willingly choose your path ahead, then you shall be forced to take a given one – and in this, the road shall indeed be long. The correct intention leads to the right manifestation. Manifesting intent is now how the way ahead shall be traversed. It will come through you, and others like you, who have taken the decision to make this highway their way. As we constantly stress – you are not alone. The world attempts to place individuals into individualistic isolated atoms of physicality – spread across the world yet not connected or unified. Separated individuals are weaker and far more easily coerced and manipulated. Yet humanity is, in reality and in practice, a collective organism – a whole, integral being. It is time now to exercise that being – to become its conscious limbs. There is individualism within unity – this is not the same as separated, individualistic elements.

Be not afraid of being a part of the whole. Some may think that it will take away their 'individual personality' – what is this anyway? Your so-called individual personality is largely a conglomerate of conditioned and programmed layers. This is the 'pseudo-self' that many have been programmed into protecting with their very lives – and unto their deaths! It is like identifying with an avatar of yourself. The path to freedom is the path to dropping the pseudo-self. There is no need to be afraid of that which you do not know. You are being afraid of ghosts. You have also been programmed from childhood to be afraid of ghosts. Remember the Bogeyman? The scary figure of your nightmares – that darkness under the bed? Outside the window? These are the tales of media excitation that have been successfully portrayed in your films and books to program the young mind against the unknown. The result is that you retreat into the safety of the known, material world. You stay away from the 'spooks' – beware of the spooky! They will take away your soul...

The security of your pseudo-self is a false security that continues to support the need for external dependencies. The more you cling to this, the more you will repel the notion of a collective being and unity. Your programmed idea of a separate individuality is a deliberate program to deny the energetic collective unity of which, in truth, you are a part.

The energy and positivity of your own localized aspect of consciousness feeds into a collective energy field that in turn forms part of the overall vibrational web of your reality. When you 'tune in,' so to speak, you are connecting and resonating with an immense resource of energy. This can be seen as the *mergence* between the physical and the energetic – of the tangible with the intangible. When this connection, this relation, between the physical and the intangible-energetic is in resonance, it is easier to manifest events within the realm of matter-reality. That is, the greater resonance between you and creative intent allows for more rapid manifestation of that intent. Therefore, it is critical to retain your positive intent and focus. And focused intent that is in alignment with the field of creative intelligence receives a greater flow of reinforcing energy. It is the same as like an antenna being in alignment with the broadcast signal. You are the antenna. Creative energy is the broadcast signal, and it seeks to be picked up and be shown – i.e., manifested – in your reality structure. As they say – Welcome to the Show!

And the Show responds, believe it or not, to your advantage. When there is an intent and desire that originates from a lower level of positivity and 'correctness,' so to say, then it makes it harder to maintain the connection and reception of signal. Imagine the difference between an antenna on stable land and an antenna at sea, on a boat, amidst a storm. Positive intention is that antenna upon land

– its foundation is fixed and stable, and its connection to the broadcast source once tuned-in is easily aligned and maintained. This is not the case for the tyranny. Those that wish to manifest powers to control are like that antenna on a boat at sea during a storm. It is more difficult to maintain connection to broadcasting energies because they have too much instability their end. They must focus and maintain attention at all times. If they lose focus, or are distracted from their plan, or things go off-plan just a tiny bit, then they lose connection with the broadcast. This is why the powers of control are so rigidly fixed and obsessed with ritual, planning, and controlled organization. They are not open to spontaneity and change and flexibility. They are not resilient in the face of change. That is why they are paranoid about straying from the status quo. They plan and plan and plan further in order to cover all their bases. They don't wish anything to disrupt their plans. The last thing they want is, as the saying goes – a spanner in the works!

This is your advantage as a human being –

you have a natural freedom, an impulsiveness. You are the Captain Kirk of Starship Earth – relying and trusting upon human instinct and gut feeling over cold logic.

The human being can run rings around the controlling forces, if truth be told. The power within each individual human being is far greater than within any number of theirs. This is why their apparatus of control must be so total and overwhelming. It must be made so that humans have almost no freedom on how to behave, think, or to be. The passivity of the human race is their only path to total control over you. This enforcement comes from the status of authority – from the obedience to uniform. This too has been well-researched and analyzed. We ask the reader to go and check on the work of Stanley Milgram – 'Obedience to Authority' – as well as to the infamous 'Stanford Prison Experiment.' The human programming to a person in uniform – or even to don the attire of a uniform – changes totally the brain patterning and functioning of a human being, so well programmed has this been in humanity.

Divide and rule is their name of the game. And this makes it much easier when people are divided between themselves. In-fighting is one of the best ways for the controllers to maintain their power. When people fight and squabble between themselves, they are giving away their power. More than this – they are sacrificing their unity. Collective resonance is disrupted when there is in-fighting between people. Look around you at your world – do you see it now? Can you see their plan?

The differences in skin color, in religious beliefs – in any beliefs! The differences in ideals, in political views, in opinion, in this, that, and the other. Difference is promoted throughout the whole world, and it begins with the early years of education. When there is great difference in front of you, you cannot see the sameness – the unity. Why cannot unity be created by a blessing and celebration of diversity?

Differences places the focus upon the magician's white rabbit – and you do not see the conjuring trick that the other hand performs. It's an ancient trick, and yet people fall for it all the time. There needs to be an awareness and awakening against this. A resistance to the overall plan of keeping humanity under a tyranny of control. The collective force of human consciousness in resonance and alignment can help to nudge their plan out of orbit just a little bit, just enough, for their whole map to be disrupted. The power of vibrational alignment is greater than you may realize. It is the power of collective perception alignment. Imagine a whole field of antennas aligned together – is not their function greatly increased? This is why you have whole fields of satellite dishes hooked up together – when they operate in alignment, they have the collective force to receive information/energy from the far reaches of the universe. Yet one satellite dish alone can do little – can receive little. These satellite dishes each exist as one separate physical unit, yet they operate together through a collective agreement. This multiplies exponentially their power. Getting to see the picture now?

It is important at the same time to observe what is going on in the world and not to shy away from seeing and knowing these things. It can be disheartening for some people to see what is unfolding in the world around them, especially as the controlling powers start increasing the roll-out of their plans. It is uncomfortable to see the increase in physical and digital surveillance, the monitoring of your lives, the enforced rituals of travel, the financial corruption, the debt bondage, the theft of your physical resources, the propaganda of the media, the exploitation of emotions, desires, and sensations, the blatant infirmity of the illness industry that they call health, the pollution of the food chain, etc, etc – this is not the place for making lists. You may know it; or you can easily go to find out more about it. The fact that you are reading these words now indicate that you are already some way down the rabbit hole, and into at least a minimal degree of awareness and awakening. Otherwise, you wouldn't have gotten this far!

By knowing their plans, this awareness helps to give you the added ability to see when the plan is both unfolding, how it is unfolding, and also when it is cracking, or when there is confusion and frustration upon their part. Observe and be aware of what is going on – yet do not get drawn into it. This is the important part – do not energetically give your focus and attention onto their events. Only coolly and calmly observe them from an energetically-protected distance. Keep your own energy resonance intact.

Be comforted that there is another plan. A plan for the greatness of the human being and a freedom from tyranny. Align yourselves with that plan.

ELEVEN

The Greater Plan for the freedom from tyranny for the human race has likewise been in play for a long, long time. Historical events are seldom as they seem! There has been a flow of creative, intelligent energies into the earth material reality for a long period of historical time. That is, there has existed, and continues to exist, an energetic source of sustenance flowing into this domain. This flow is highly coordinated and flows with intelligence. An awareness and acknowledgement of this flow offers a great resource to each person. This is the presence of intentional energy that is more potent than the intentional energy of lower vibrations. The situation now is one of awareness. By knowing more about the agenda for controlling humanity, you can be aware of when things are going to plan and when things are not. In those moments of disruption, slowdown or, as we say, a hiccup, then focused concentration can be placed onto those areas to disrupt them further and take them off-plan. Never doubt the power of concentrated focus and awareness.

In the grander scheme of things, these current events to further control the consciousness of humanity is itself a 'hiccup' within the overall trajectory of human evolution. It will, in time, be seen as a catalyst that was used to accelerate the awakening of humanity. Their dark plans can be used as a tool for your own advancement in perception and cognition. The planners of control like to say – 'never let a good crisis go to waste.' Well, we can say this too! And within the larger scheme of things, we have the upper hand. It will be good to focus on this as events become more turbulent for a time.

It should be remembered that chaos fuels greater change. It is stagnation that can be more harmful. It is more difficult to instigate evolvement and transition in times of great stillness and balance. Of course, balance is very necessary within the collective resonance, and energetically – yet balance within the physical domain lacks certain triggers and impulses for accelerated movement. It is the same when driving a car. When you need to go faster you must press your foot down harder upon the accelerator pedal. This allows more fuel to pass into the engine which in turn allows greater speed. If you wish to overtake another car, it takes much longer when you are driving at a stable speed – it can seem like it takes almost forever! And if you don't hurry up then you will be in the way of the oncoming traffic and possibly for a head-on collision. So, what is necessary in this moment to pass onto the road ahead of the car? You need to press the foot to the pedal – 'step on the gas' as they say – and accelerate the movement. Do you see this? Chaos and turbulence form a necessary trigger for acceleration in such moments of potential danger such as overtaking another car. Humanity has entered into an 'overtaking phase' right now. Prepare for a moment of speed – of necessary acceleration. And again, as they say – fasten seatbelts!

The possibility and opportunity for awareness is available to all people equally. What you have gained in perception is possible for others too – yet it is a question of choice. If others, such as your friends, family, colleagues, etc, do not have this awareness, it is because they have chosen not to seek it. There is no elitism in awareness. Human consciousness is the property of all human beings. The decisions taken on how to use, develop, and expand access to consciousness is an individual choice. Do not feel bad for others if they do not share your awareness, or if they worry and fear about things that you do not. You may find this troubling – but you cannot give them perception. No more than you can live their life for them. Perception is an always-on, always-available potentiality and resource. It is never closed – it cannot be.

The engagement with conscious perceptions and awareness opens up the possibility for further insights and awareness – it is like an expanding feedback loop. Greater access to this awareness also provides more insight into the 'bigger picture' of all that is unfolding. The human predicament is but one aspect within this huge tapestry. This tapestry operates within various dimensions and in a non-linear way that a normal, unprepared consciousness cannot fathom. It is for this reason that a prepared consciousness, or cognitive perception, is necessary from a purely functional point of view. To repeat – conscious awareness is not some type of elite club. It is for everyone. It is just that the minimal cost of admission is reaching it. Once you get there – you're in!

As processes within the grander scheme are not linear, they may, from an external perspective, be regarded as somewhat chaotic. It should be stressed here that chaos can also act as an energy-attractor, like a vortex of energy. Again, to use the analogy of overtaking another car. As has been said, it is necessary to press down the accelerator to gain more speed. Also required will be a change in gear. Whether manual or automatic, the car will need to shift into a gear most appropriate for the necessary burst of acceleration. When the car (the gear stick) is within any one of its positions, then it can be said to be stable. The car will operate within the speed limits of that particular gear. When the gear stick is taken out of gear, then before it can be repositioned in its new state, it will temporarily be in a 'chaotic node.' That is, it is in-between states and neither one nor the other. It is therefore not linear and open to unpredictable energies. Yet it is that in-between state – the transition state – that is needed to jump into a new, more stable position. This is how the car functions as it moves along. The gear position is being shifted continuously, from 1 to 2 to 3 to 4 to 3 again, to 2, to 3 to 4 to 5 to 4 to 2 ..etc, etc….. this continual re-shifting and repositioning is necessary in order to coordinate the overall trajectory of car, its driver, and maybe its passengers, to their destination. From a micro perspective, this may seem like a non-linear, chaotic, and turbulent way to make a journey. Yet from the overall grander perspective, it appears that the car and its passengers have had a smooth journey. Furthermore, the passengers would have completed their journey much faster than if they had remained within one gear only, trundling along at a snail's pace.

What this tells you is that the ups and downs, the swings in and out of chaotic nodes, are actually what fuels the dramatic unfolding of the larger journey. Isn't that amazing?

When we now observe strict and rigid protocols of order, what we see is restraint, confinement, and the imposed blockages against evolvement. Now do you see more clearly the plans for the controlled confinement of humanity? The need to control every movement, every transaction, every thought, every purchase, every glance on the web – in all, every aspect of a person's life. This is a form of control bordering on the obsessive. Such obsession also shows a paranoia against the whims of flow and uncertainty.

Agreement to combat the tyranny against consciousness is also an agreement to visualize and focus conscious intent upon the creative flow of this planet and its energies. That is, to focus intent against the controlling forces of rigidity and ritualized organization. Your own aligned resonance of conscious awareness is a commitment to counter-act the forces of tyranny. Aligning your creative intent is itself a blockage to their plans of human confinement. Do not think that such a non-tangible, nonvisible thing as consciousness has no power. This is what 'they' wish you to believe. In fact, it is the very source of power itself – and always has been. Time now to tap into this! It is time now to step up into service.

If you are reading this, then it is very likely you have already committed to be of service before you became consciously aware of it. You came here to be of service. Until now you have been dressed within a robe and role of obscurity, beneath the radar. Time now to allow your consciousness to expand and participate in this great game to defeat tyranny. Time now to be a conduit force.

PART TWO

'Much of the mendacity which exists in the world
today serves the purpose of rocking people to sleep
so that they do not see the reality, are deflected from
reality, and the spirits of darkness have it all their
own way with the human race. All kinds of things are
falsely presented to people to deflect them from truths
they could experience if they were awake and, indeed,
ought to experience, if human evolution is to proceed
in a fruitful way. This is the age when human beings
must take affairs into their own hands.'

Rudolf Steiner – 28 October 1917

TWELVE

'The devil pales beside the man who owns a
truth, *his* truth.'
Emile Cioran

Every human being has the right to express
and manifest their magnificent heritage.
Within them, and through them, flows an
energy and power that would surprise each
person if they were awake to it. Humanity
represents one aspect of life within a life-
filled cosmos of incredible intelligence. Yet
knowledge, and also access, to this larger
reality has been blocked to the human species.
Humanity has long lived within a form of
cosmic quarantine. For this reason, humanity
has long believed it is alone – a lone species
within the vast, cosmic neighborhood, both

near and endlessly far. This sense of solitude has been instilled within the human mind as a form of deceptive programming. The truth is far more wonderful. Humanity exists as part of a cosmic family of life – yet knows this not. For now.

The practice of deception and bondage over humanity is coming to an end. It has been decided, on behalf of humanity, from those who have the best interests of humanity in mind. There are far more players in this Bigger Game than many realize. There are many players from afar. Not everything revolves around the limited spectrum of the human senses. Humanity needs to have some faith in those things that are presently unknown to them. Not everything is immediate. People have become too accustomed to having everything presented before them. This is the fallacy of the material paradigm. Everything can be seen, known, and tested. And from this, a series of reactions are established. For far too long, humanity in general has been in reactive mode to material events and objects. They should take a lesson from the indigenous people of this planet. Observe calmly and quietly from an inner perspective – *allow* some of the knowing to seep through you bodily, as the intuition disperses through your receptors. Receive and consider – instead of always *seeing* and *reacting*.

In these current times it will be important to cultivate this *inner distance* within you. This creates a 'buffer' zone between external events and impacts, and your immediate reaction to them. Think of this as a 'pause' mode whereby you do not allow yourself to react immediately to any given impact. There is a time-lapse period where the usual 'event-impact-reaction' structure is slowed down. Within this slowed period, allow yourself time to digest, observe, and consider what is happening. Only after this, allow yourself to give a *response*. This is not the same as making a reaction.

When the unfolding events are only seen through the material perspective, then it may appear that the situation is more negative than it may be. That is why there has been an ongoing effort to dull the perceptivity of human consciousness. The controlling powers do not want for people to perceive beyond the façade of material events. There is a curtain that prevents you from seeing what is going on behind. Remember the analogy of this in the famous film *The Wizard of Oz*? The fearful, projected face of the Great Wizard booms out loud causing fear reactions in people. And when Dorothy's small dog – Toto – pulls back the curtain, the old, jittery man is seen pulling the levers. This is exactly how it is. The curtain has been pulled over you...and now it is being pulled away.

There are many surprises in store for humanity in these coming years. Before the curtain shall be pulled away, first there will be rips. And through these rips, people will see the illusion and façade, like wool pulled over your eyes, being dropped. Some of what has been going on behind the scenes will be made public. Many well-known people will be humiliated. Many well-regarded institutions will lose face and their reputation. This will be a time for patience and observation. Change is coming. Yet it will neither be linear nor obvious change.

A new form of experience is coming to life upon the planet. Before this comes, there will be disruptive events in the normal way of living. Do not overtly fight these or struggle with them. Do not consider the use of physical force. Your power is not within physical force – it is beyond that. Do not fall into the trap of playing *their* game. This is your game too – but you must understand and play by *your* rules.

This, however, also requires your participation. The individual needs to be willing to allow this new experience to manifest. You, the reader, must call it in. Long-standing deceptions have rooted into you from many generations of deliberate programming. You must not act from these places of deception – this is the unwelcome *reactive* mode. Do not act from a place of automation. First, you need to make a conscious decision to change your life experience. A person must be willing to commit to a newer perspective – a different cognitive perception that is free from imposed conditioning. This must first be asked for from yourselves. The choice must be given – and given willingly from the heart of yourself.

Only then can a chain of experiential events be set in motion. Everything is a matter of choice – make this *your choice*. Do not allow others to make choices on your behalf. Especially choices that are not in your favor. Begin to live your own truths.

Living from your own truths, your own commitment to a change in experience, these will initiate a different flow of energy into your lives. Remember those universal laws that underly the human experience for they reflect a grander reality – energy attracts like energy. Find those things that resonate with you, that enhance your energy state, and nurture those connections. Do not throw away energy uselessly. As it was said by the great Teacher Jeshua/Jesus - *Do not give what is holy to the dogs; nor cast your pearls before swine.*

The broader spectrum of energy supports those things that remain in alignment, in resonance, with cosmic principles. Support, therefore, those actions that are in alignment with the furtherance of positive intentions. Those factions – the elite controlling cult – will find their plans being withdrawn of energy. It will become more and more difficult for them to energetically sustain their actions and planned events. Because of this, they shall turn to panic and acts of desperation. This may begin with using brute force – and human puppets – to enforce their plans rather than through stealth and more subtle means. Whilst this may seem uncomfortable in the beginning, it will actually work against them for it will help in showing to the world, to the general populace, what are their true intentions. They will no longer be able to hide behind walls of clever and slick deception. The plan for the control of humanity and the tyranny against human consciousness will be laid upon the table for others to see. This will create a more even playing field. More attention will then arrive upon such messages as these, and such people as yourselves, who are promoting a shift to a new consciousness of perception. An energetic momentum will be created and will expand. Consciousnesses in resonance result in exponential growth. People will begin to find each other as if from nowhere. New relations will begin as online connections between likeminded-energy people are established. New networks will emerge.

There shall be renewed growth from the bottom-up. Decentralization shall be the advantage to people once the weaknesses in the centralized plan of the controllers is evident. Accumulation of awareness can become the chink in their armor. Their arrogance does not permit them to recognize this.

Accumulation of awareness will also help to disseminate information about their plan – the plan of tyranny over humanity. The spread of information will help in raising awareness which will then result in further spread of information. Humans will inform other humans. The awakening will grow within the collective consciousness of humanity, allowing others to tap into and receive these 'intuitions' with greater ease. You yourselves – collective humanity – shall become your own communication channel. You will be a living body of knowledge between yourselves.

As this awareness grows, more and more people will remove their participation from the controller's plan. More people will withdraw their support and belief in it, and acceptance shall dwindle. Under the weight of withdrawing support and growing condemnation and criticism, the great plan is likely to collapse. Humanity can bring this about. In fact, this is your mission – a mission plan for the human species. First, it begins with the few. It has always begun with the few. Do not be disheartened by numbers. Energy does not count – and cannot be counted upon fingers. Energy works by intent.

Grow your intention.

THIRTEEN

There is a Greater Plan of which it is almost impossible to describe. Only a direct perception of it can give indication of the scale and complexity. The perception that belongs to the majority of humanity is a very closed and limited spectrum perception. This will need to be expanded now as part of the process of the species' evolutionary progress. Great things are coming, once this transitional hiccup can be overcome. The Greater Plan is a wholly positive one that belongs to a cosmic collective of intelligence. Those who wish to control the planet have a 'lesser plan' that aims for restriction, constriction, and containment of human consciousness. This is a grand tyranny. The positive approach is always one of expansion and growth. Those elements or events that restrict and constrain consciousness always belong to a negative approach. It is high time now for humanity to break out of this *consciousness quarantine* and to perceive aspects of the Greater Plan. There is a wealth of cosmic wonder that awaits for human participation. There is much assistance for humanity to gain this freedom. However, as it has been stated – humanity must *choose* this direction and commit to it. The Greater Plan for the freedom and expansion of human consciousness cannot be imposed, despite it being of positive intention. The path of freedom must itself be a choice – just as the path of enslavement has been a willing choice of humanity as a result of the great deceptions and illusions fostered upon the planet.

As the gameplay becomes more visible, more people shall awaken. This is because there are people who have been awaiting a triggering. They perhaps did not know it, yet there are aspects within them that 'sense' the larger truth and only need certain external events of magnitude to knock away the dusty layers of delusion. Many who have not yet known of this shall be called forth. Again, there is not contest or battle in numbers – it is a question of intent and the clarity of the energies behind this intent. The intent for the negative path works through fear – fear of being caught out. It is a fear of being discovered, and so they rush ahead with the plan. It is similar to the tale of the vampires who rush around at night, in the dark, before they have to scuttle back again to their castles, dark caves or coffins, before the dawn. These creatures are powerful and strong within the dark yet turn to dust within a single blade of light. Their power resides within their darkness and the fear they project onto others. Likewise, the same can be said for the controllers of this planet. They seem all-powerful within these 'dark nights' yet they are scurrying and rushing around for fear that dawn may appear before their plans are fully in place. YOU should not be fearing.

YOUR power is that you exist within the full Light – the full light of the day. At the same time, you can enter into the dark without worry. The night-time is also a place where you can wander without harm. The human being can walk through the light and the dark and remain unharmed. The negative entities live only within their own darkness. This is a great weakness for them, and they know it. As their plan unfolds, they will have to step more into the light in order to enact it. This light will give more visibility to their agenda. It will be hard for their plans to stay in the dark, as it has in the past.

You see now why the 'real' dark players of this controlling cult are unknown within the public domain? They use public figures as puppets for their plans. They have to stay in the dark – they are afraid of the light. The light is your power. The information highway network of the Internet can be used to do more research and to uncover their trails. They are afraid of this also. This is one of the reasons why they wish to control, restrict – or even shut down – parts of the Internet as they know it can be a useful and powerful tool within the hands of the people. There is a struggle here to control this digital domain too. Luckily for you, there are many humans who are technologically savvy and intelligent in this area and also have awareness of some of these darker plans. Some of them are called as 'hackers' and they too are in service to humanity. Not all of them – yet enough. They are networking and collaborating and have been doing so for some time. They are also coming more to the fore and expanding their ranks. Their presence will be necessary for what shall come to pass.

The intention to change the current gameplay can be successful – never doubt this. Once this is understood, the commitment to changing the gameplay becomes easier. Once committed, a new energy of consciousness opens to you. This is not magic nor lies. New pathways of intention first need to be established. The energy of consciousness cannot flow into a closed vessel. Therefore, it is important that understanding and acceptance then leads to commitment. Are you committed to the plan of awakening?

Knowledge, understanding, commitment, and intention are powerful tools in the hands of those who know how to wield them. Do not doubt the power of such 'intangible tools.' They may not be the visible tools you are used to wielding as a species – such as rocks and guns – yet these are the more powerful tools for bringing down the opposition that you now face. Recognize this – accept it. Do not doubt it.

Intention working together in coherence and commitment towards evolvement attains much. And more so, unlike the physical tools you so much like to hold in your hands – these tools cannot be taken away from you. They become a part of You – if you allow and accept them. Isn't that a positive thought to consider?

FOURTEEN

The necessary change will not come about through physical resistance. This is an important aspect to understand. As tempting as it will be in certain situations to react in a form of physical protest or rebellion – bear in mind that this is *exactly* how the controllers will be expecting you to respond. And they will have planned for this and have resources at hand to both combat and respond in return. This has been mentioned previously and will no doubt be mentioned again, as repetition will help to reinforce this understanding.

You have been programmed to think in terms of 'fighting fire with fire.' This was also a reaction-response that had some utility at different times in the past. Consciousness was not yet developed enough to bring forth the power of conscious awareness and focused intention. Nor was the planet sufficiently connected and networked to bring together like-minds. In past situations, a physical response was necessary and, at times, the only option. There were other ways too that involved much planning, organization, and patient arrangement. Always as there are overt, external events – so too are there equally events that go unnoticed to the general masses and which operate, as they say, below the radar. Now, however, there is the potential for a mass participation and involvement. Mass consciousness can align itself with physical networks as well as energetic ones to bring about a highly amplified correspondence of energies and intentions.

For many people, a lack of knowing purpose for being here on this planet has left them debilitated. A lack of knowledge regarding purpose – as well as origins – is a form of deliberate amnesia fostered upon the human race as part of their containment and restriction of perception. Do not allow this to pull you back or diminish your energies. Your purpose is not a single straight line or a single thing. Your purpose, in one regard, is simply to experience and *to have experiences*. You do not always need to 'do' in order to 'be' for you already ARE. Allow yourselves to be this.

Yet there are purposes within purposes, just as there are dolls within dolls in your Russian Doll analogy and physical object. One of your purposes may very well be to awaken within this lifetime experience – have you ever considered this? If you are drawn to these messages, then you may be one of those persons who have planned - or put into deed of purpose – the intention of awakening during these times on this planet. If this is so, then your time is NOW. This is your trigger – and this can be your awakening. Do not take such things lightly. Yet do not consider them heavy either. There is no weight. Instead, there is an opening.

Do not let frustration to enter into this opening in the first moments. Allow acceptance and gratitude to flood in. Gratitude that you are here now and that you came here for now. Within the great complexity of life, you have allowed for so many parts to come together now for this. Isn't that magical? You are a part of this wonderful planning too. You were counting on yourself to be here now. And you arrived just in time.

When your understanding and thinking come together at this time, when you consider the content of these messages, a shift will occur within you. Purpose is not only something that one assigns to the life of the physical body upon this planet. A greater purpose comes back into awareness for you. There is great purpose in this expanding awareness. Welcome to the club. Welcome to yourself. Purpose can be found within each lifetime, yet it may not be only a lifetime purpose – it may also form part of multiple lifetimes. Your purpose may be ongoing – only that you needed to discover it *within this lifetime* in order for you to continue as planned.

FIFTEEN

Do not think that you need to be 'clever' in order to recognize this tyranny against you, or doubt that perhaps you are not educated enough to grasp the implications here. This is in fact the very contrary of what you need. Cleverness is not knowledge or understanding. What your society deems as cleverness is an ability to work logically with the tools that have been programmed into your cultures. At your schools and places of education, the 'clever' person was the one who could best regurgitate the 'facts' – or rather, the disseminated information – and display either a mimicry of the information or capacity to juggle the information within the parameters of your conditioned thinking. This is neither knowledge, comprehension, nor wisdom. Cleverness is an ability to show conformity to a high degree of acceptance of narrative structures and conditioned thinking patterns. Is this what you really want to achieve?

Likewise, the 'educated person' is the one most completely imbued with the conditioned thinking of their time – and the ability to express this within the similarly confined thinking of their peers. Cleverness is not required here. Clever people need not apply.

We need free thinkers. Here, within these messages, each reader will find material that will assist in the deconditioning process. A certain, minimal level of deconditioning is necessary in order to perceive the lower level of the tyranny against human consciousness. Once this tyranny can be perceived for what it is, then it begins to lose its hold over you. From there, a person can move through and beyond the spectrum of perception confinement.

To repeat, do not consider cleverness or education as a necessity for perceiving the tyranny. The very opposite is required, for the educational structure and apparatus is the very means for upholding the tyranny. You do not need to bring your baggage here. Leave it all at the front door. Bring yourself, and a willingness to have many other things drop away from you. Don't bring fear, anxiety, or apprehension. Know that you have everything you need right where you are. You were always carrying everything that you ever needed – only that it has been hidden from you. It was hidden from all of you. Every person has had to take off, peel away, the layers of delusion that congealed over you like a rubber wetsuit, like a second skin of illusion that did not allow your pores of perception to breath correctly. Time to take off this conditioned skin and to breathe again. This is where it begins – with this acceptance and willingness. With an openness. Not with an educated mind or a suit of social acceptability. The first necessity for entry into fuller perception is Lightness. Bring your Lightness. Leave the heaviness behind way, way before you even get to the door.

Much has been talked about too of the intellect. The intellectual faculty has been fairly recent in human beings, relatively speaking. People in the far past did not 'think' in the way people do today. It was a critical function of the brain. It helped to organize and analyze. The intellect was never to be associated with the human imagination. Now, everything is clumped together within the human mind – it's all one big messy lump. The intellect was pushed to the fore in modern society and the imaginative faculties driven into retreat. Those people who exercised the imaginative faculty were accused as being 'daydreamers.' It was a derogatory term, used to herd people into a dominant intellect caging. Why? Because it is much easier to control the narrative when disseminated through the intellect mode. The tyranny is about making an absurd reality into a logical acceptance. It is largely through the intellect that this has been established. The absurdity of modern society with its inequalities, financial irregularities, and the political shenanigans parading as democracy are all surreal fragments. Yet they can be pieced together as 'reasonable' when they appeal to the linear, myopic organizing principle of the intellect. Is it 'reasonable' that governments talk about printing trillions of dollars when the governments neither own their own money systems nor is there any physical reality to a 'trillion dollars'? It is a surreal fantasy that gets played out by binary digits that don't in actuality exist. This is the illusion of much of this world – it does not in actuality exist. Nor can it. It is a game narrative – a storyboard. It is very similar to a film script that is being written by an author on their machine whilst the actors hear the author's words in their heads. This is how it is. They even made a comedy film about this very situation – yet who was laughing at who?

The human intellect can take all these separate, disjointed parts and collate them all together into a more coherent whole. This is what the intellect is good at – making a logical picture from disjointed pieces. And this helps the controllers to throw so much contrasting and dissimilar things into the mix. There is a part of the human mind that *feels* this disjuncture and senses that something is not quite right. Yet the intellect makes a logical excuse and reasoning; it is very successful at persuading the semi-conscious mind into accepting this. Yet the slight disjoint between actuality and illusion is just enough to cause a fissure of cognitive dissonance within the human mind. It is within this state of permanent low resonance cognitive dissonance that keeps the human mind open and vulnerable to brainwashing and programming. The tyranny against human consciousness is that the human being is kept within an either/or polarity state through this constant unsettled zone of dissonance. Such dissonance creates mental discomfort. If this state of mental discomfort continues for long enough, the person's ability to correctly perceive or maintain stable perspectives is damaged. In order to reduce this discomfort and restore balance, which is the natural functioning of mental cognition, then the brain will choose a state – such as between the binary 0 or 1 – and settle into that state. The option 'most comfortable' is the dominant consensus narrative. It is because of this that most people find security and comfort within their society's general consensus. To slip outside of this dominant narrative often initiates the original discomfort of dissonance, so people quickly return to their 'set point' – the consensus narrative. This technique keeps the majority of people within a pre-programmed spectrum that is maintained and adjusted accordingly by the controllers of this tyranny. It is brutal and shows that they, the controllers, are the ones who operate through a cold-blooded cleverness that is not capable of compassion or genuine comprehension.

That is why it may initially feel discomforting to break away from the social conditioning. Yet the person needs to persist with this, and not to easily succumb to the temptation to return to 'set point.' A new equilibrium must be sought and maintained. Once that new equilibrium of cognitive perception is set, there is not only no more dissonance discomfort, there is a complete detoxification from the older frequency programming. Just like 'going clean' in terms of physical-bodily addiction, so the cognitive state is cleared of its need for conditioned security. And there is never any need to go back.

It is time for the human being to return to their centeredness – a state of coherence, on so many levels.

SIXTEEN

This state of dislocation as previously mentioned has also been utilized for the grander narratives of human origin and the story of the gods. There has been a perpetual strategy to keep humanity in ignorance about its origin, its connection with the cosmos, and further truths about humanity's innate potential and power. In order to quench this longing for comprehension that resides within each human, various ideologies were selected and put forth as 'truth narratives' when the reality was that they were ideologies of illusion. The discrepancies and differences between these various 'grand narratives' also served to further the dissonance amongst humans and to also create divides that ran deep into their societies. These so-called 'religious differences' have been utilized time and time again to create diversion, chaos, and in-fighting. There are several purposes that can be taken from human in-fighting, one of them being as a distraction technique from the real agenda that advances in the background.

There have been many interventions of wisdom into human civilization. Some of these have been operated through specific individuals that then put forth and disseminated certain wisdom teachings. These teachings contained knowledge of this tyrannical situation – the real human condition – often in veiled or disguised forms so as to maintain for as long as possible the transmission potential of the channel. However, in the majority of cases, these initial transmissions were hijacked, distorted, and then manipulated by the controllers in order to further serve their agenda of human enslavement. Some of these transmissions still retain veiled traces of original content - if a person can either decode or resonate with this information. On the whole, these transmission teachings no longer serve humanity in their need for advancement and can be left alone. Do not use these distorted teachings as a reason to seek validation for further human division. To do so would be to continue to play into the hands of your own imprisonment.

Another use of these distorted grand narratives has been to program people to give away their power to external sources. Not only were people subjugated to 'gods in the sky' who watched and lorded over them, but then later this instigated the rise of priestly classes who formed a physical, earthly set of institutions to further regulate the masses. These 'middle regulators' also served as power links in the chain, and again persuaded people to give over their natural rights to any internal connection to their own power. In short, people were conditioned into believing that they could not form any valid or truthful connection within or through themselves with Greater Intelligence. These grand religious narratives helped in strengthening the slave mentality that has persisted to modern day. People have allowed others to lord it over them quite literally, as lords and ladies of elite families and the monarchy continue to reign over their 'loyal subjects.' There is a revolution coming in human consciousness that will change the whole social landscape. Part of the advancement in human cognition entails understanding the power that has been exercised over humanity by the creation of artificial social hierarchies.

These grand religious narratives have also been utilized to foster and inculcate a stream of *victim consciousness* into the mass collective mind of humanity. The conflating of the act of prayer with the notion of begging was a deliberate mix. Rather than asking for personal empowerment, the prayer was enacted as a form of relief. This served to alleviate people rather than enabling and energizing them. This psychological state of victimhood has now been indoctrinated into the mental, emotional, and physical conditioning within humanity and needs to be dropped. The human has only been a victim through enforced ignorance. And this is now coming to an end. Time to shift into encouraging the emergence of the power within each human individual to make the choice to take responsibility for themselves in this new world. It is time to choose responsibility. YOU are not a victim.

Consider it more as a projection. Those people and groups in control fear losing their own power. They are victims to themselves. Yet they also fear admitting this and cannot face the reality of their own weakness. It makes them feel strong to project and deflect this weakness and victimhood onto you – the people. When you accept this weakness and parade this publicly, it makes them feel good and emboldened. They feel that they were right all along to think of humans as weak and victims – but this is THEIR delusion. They have been deluding themselves by making humans act this out for their behalf. Do not be these false actors. Do not be their stooges. It is time for the controllers of this tyranny to recognize and face their own weakness. They are also in ignorance of this. In fact, they have been in greater ignorance for they have known of this and yet sought to cover it up, to actively deny it. Yet human beings have been placed within an innocent ignorance – unknowingly and therefore willingly.

Ignorance cannot be utilized into knowledge.

Certain 'correct' or truthful forms of experiences can be distilled into knowledge and then, with further distillation, into wisdom. It is the natural heritage of humankind to have a broad range of experiences that can then be used for gaining knowledge, insight, understanding, and eventually wisdom. This is a universal pattern that many species undergo. Yet here, upon this planet, the controlled nature has disrupted this flow of truthful experiences. Thus, a form of naturally occurring wisdom has been blocked from the evolutionary stream on this planet. This has greatly debilitated the awakening and perceptive advancement of humankind. Misleading information and deliberately deceptive knowledge have made the 'wisdom experience' extremely difficult. For this reason, it has been a closely guarded path for initiates over the many generations of historical time. It has been a heavily protected secret that had to guard itself against the persecution of the controllers. Does the Inquisition and the burning of the great library of Alexandria now give more meaning to you?

Humanity now has to take the responsibility

for demanding and creating their truthful experiences. Humanity has the potential for much greater understanding. This potentiality is reason enough for gaining access. Do not allow the ignorance to continue. Make the decision within your own center of being – within your own knowingness. Take the decision and draw those experiences to you that you need. Draw them to you through energetic resonance. You no longer need to be at the whim of events, as flotsam floats upon the sea.

Do not go gentle into that good night – these are words from the poet Dylan Thomas. Take heed of these words. Take them into you. Do not accept to walk into the end days of your life if you have not yet first awoken. What life has there been if you were asleep through all your days, only to awaken after death? Do not go gentle into that good night – awaken dear soul. Awaken into that good Light.

SEVENTEEN

Many have walked amongst humankind that have known of the truth of the human condition. It was a truth that was a burden as well as a liberation. Those that spoke too openly and directly were persecuted. Others spoke in riddles, in parables, in occult forms and variations. The true knowledge of the human condition has always existed in some form upon the planet. Such streams of this knowledge were kept well protected - this was necessary. At times this was thought of as elitist by others that could not understand. This was not so. It is only that each person must become their own price of admission. If you cannot reach at least to the front door, then how can you expect the door to open? The door does not come to where you are. Each person must accomplish the minimum of travel to arrive at the threshold. There is then a crossing available at the threshold. Yet do not expect a taxi service from your own sofa or front door of your own dwelling place. Your entitlement must be earned. It is yours, and you have the right to declare your entitlement. Yet it still must be earned. For if it is not, it remains packed in a box with layers of tape over it.

The knowledge was protected because otherwise it would become distorted. It is very clear that this has been the case in most known examples that exist in the world. Whether within religions, personal revelations or wayshowers – so much of the messages have been hijacked and turned into the dust of their original message. More than this, in many instances the messages have been converted into programming traps – the very opposite of their original function. The underground or indirect nature of this transmission of knowledge in past ages has been noted – it was for a very good, specific reason. Now that necessity has passed. The degree of conscious awareness, cognition, and the capacity to interpret available information has shifted how these messages can now be offered. That is, there is now a more advanced level of general cognition across the planet since the human species consciousness has shifted in vibration. There is now more access to the consciousness field, making it possible for more people to 'receive' insights. This is how innovation, creative vision, and imaginative thought becomes expressed and actualized – through this contact. This level of contact across the species is now more widespread and 'accessible.' Further, there is now the 'language context' available to better frame this knowledge. There is less need for riddles and parables. The lexicon of conditioning, programming, and cognitive perception is now more widely known – thanks to the language of psychology, computing, and other subjects. There is now a widespread vocabulary for expressing the interior world of humankind and its processes. Likewise, there are analogies – such as within your technologies – for how parts of the system (program) act and behave and are programmed. The knowledge of humankind can now be expressed in the open – in broad daylight, as you say. Therefore, messages such as these will continue to arrive in many ways, through many channels/vessels, and will be seen embedded within many formats.

These messages have also been embedded, or encrypted, within media outlets. They have been unconsciously 'channeled' by creative people – often unknowingly – into many formats over past years. This includes within popular novels and films. You may recognize them more when you return and 're-discover' these encrypted art forms. Some of the messages are more direct than others, according to certain specifics of each expression. These ongoing transmissions have helped to prepare the 'mental soil' for this time. The human mind is now more attuned to this information. Through these ongoing transmissions, the mind of humanity has been gradually re-wired so that heightened perceptions will find a more fertile soil to develop within.

The controllers on this planet have recognized this development within the cognitive advancement of humanity. Their scheming is now finding it more difficult to maintain the illusion of reality that has been established. For this reason, they have also increased their endeavors and have introduced several new agendas to advance their own plans. One of these is the increased control and manipulation of mainstream media and news sources. The other is the deliberate dissemination of misinformation and the infiltration of alternative media organizations. Surveillance is also at an all-time high and is now almost pervasive. This agenda is now focused to expand to the next, complete and total control level if nothing is done to curtail this project. Many are working across this planet, and elsewhere, to combat this increased control over the surveillance spectrum.

Human consciousness is increasing its own spectrum radiance/vibration, and this has advanced considerably more than most people are consciously aware of. This cannot, and should not, be underestimated in its potential to change the future outcomes. Human perception is piercing through more of the veil of illusion. The cracks in the perception bubble are increasingly showing. The controllers will now need to 'up their game' with great speed if they are to counteract the advancement in perceptive cognition amongst people. This they have already done, which has led in part to the transmission of these particular messages. Yet it is to be recognized that in their rapid response, the controllers are in a rushed phase. This can, we expect, lead to some mistakes being made. One of these is that their plans now have to be made more public and visible. Visibility is not something that the controllers favor. On the contrary, they have tried with immense resources to remain behind the scenes. The acknowledgement of their presence is one of their own greatest fears. Yet speed and subtlety do not always go together within a physical matter-reality. The more a timeline is advanced artificially, the more it becomes seen and thus recognized. Greater visibility on the part of the tyranny is now coming to the fore. This is to the advantage of humanity.

It is important that humanity thus

acknowledges its own state of mental, emotional, and 'spiritual' captivity that has taken place. So much information and true knowledge have been hidden from you. Before moving beyond your present state, it is necessary to recognize what have been your chains. For so long, these chains were seen to be 'deserved' because of humankind's lowly position before some great-almighty god. This was yet another form of mastery over you. This imposed mentality of being 'lowly creatures' before the 'supreme creator' is a narrative so corrosive that it needs to be shredded immediately. Little can be done so long as this narrative fills up space within you. The 'All-Controlling God' is a fantasy program that has been at the center of the controlling narrative for so long. It has been a successful narrative across the recent civilizations of this planet. It served also to perpetuate specific social and political hierarchical systems used to socially manage the populace. It is deeply embedded within the collective historical memory – yet it has been reduced greatly over recent years to the point where it no longer holds central place and its ability to function as a programming device-narrative is albeit finished. This will shift a tremendous energy of power over to people themselves. The knowledge and recognition of the 'god-seed' within each person will serve to empower humanity. This is a very necessary step for the upcoming phases of human evolution.

Self-awareness is arising within the individual. This gives the ability to 'individualize' oneself away from the mass herd programming. This self-awareness will resonate with and attract greater intuitive awareness. This can then develop and expand the awareness beyond a linear fashion. Realization and understanding are exponential, not incremental. The greater the self-awareness within the individual, the harder it will be to exploit and manipulate them. The individual will develop in their ability to decide and choose the type of life experiences they wish to encounter. That is, each person will increasingly manifest those experiences they *consciously will* into being. These experiences will then serve to advance the individual's perception. This perception will then resonate and attract further realizations and expand the perceptive bubble, or spectrum, of the individual. It is an expanding series of feedback processes aimed at allowing each person to become the driver towards their own realization. No external power is necessary to bring understanding and realization. It has been part of humanity's own legacy and inheritance that people contain within themselves the resources for their own advancement – *if they choose.*

The ability to choose has been deliberately distorted and erased through increasing and invasive social programming in human societies. The ability to choose manifested reality was relegated to 'occult matters' and driven from the mainstream narratives in your cultures. People were trained to stay within specific parameters and confines of perception. Those who strayed beyond these confines and exercised certain perceptive faculties often ended up on fires or within dungeons. Freedom of expression was seldom tolerated. This has been the tyranny against consciousness upon the planet. Acknowledge and accept this. Own this portion of your history. When you own it, you can move beyond it without damage. Own now too your responsibility to advance your cognition and conscious awareness. It is YOURS – it has always been yours. For a long time, your species did not know this. That time has passed. Everything is coming into the open now.

Wisdom gained will provide those experiences for more understanding. It is like shifting the angle of the camera lens just slightly – a new perspective comes into view. It is not necessary for a grand shift to be made at once. Just a small difference in inclination will bring a different picture into view. If the camera lens moves toward the light, brighter colors will come into focus to color the scene and thus gives a different look to the complete picture. Likewise, if the camera is moved toward where there is more darkness, the overall picture will appear darkened and more enclosed. If the lens is then reduced further, the viewing parameter of the picture is lessened. This can continue until only a small dot is finally seen. All perceptions are then derived only from within this small dot of where the camera lens has been focused.

This is the same with human consciousness. The tyranny has artificially reduced the scope of human vision through deliberate programs to 'dumb down' the populace. Social and educational systems; contrived and manipulated information; distorted forms of knowledge; engineered propaganda – the human sphere of conscious awareness has been treated as their playground.

Yet now the camera lens is turning to where there is more light. The aperture is widening, the focus is drawing back. A bigger picture is coming into view, with more color and greater parameters. The spectrum of human consciousness is widening. Are you ready for empowering the new picture coming into view? Welcome to this time – to YOUR time.

EIGHTEEN

Despite the seeming confusions, there is clarity to be gained. Clarity comes from direct perception – what is also known as the direct-intuitive mode. This is the individual's own connection through their personal perceptive faculties. If this was not the case, then there would be a thousand mixed truths, and more, running amok, claiming sovereignty. The confusion, and the multiple false-truths, all belong to the lower spectrum of dense, physical awareness and 'social consciousness' (aka, social conditioning). When a person gains direct access to knowledge, this is known immediately and is not controversial. Neither is it debatable. Debates occur in external, subjective contexts. People who have awoken to the truths do not debate them. Nor are they likely to speak of them openly, for speaking is also mainly utilized by those whom do not know. When a person knows, there is no compulsion to proclaim. Proclaiming is left for the lesser truths.

These messages are not the truth, nor do they claim to be the truth. What they are, and what their function is, is to direct a person towards their own path of finding the truths for themselves. Each person is their own teacher. Yet because of the accumulation of conditioned junk and programmed biases that have been pushed onto people from controlling agendas, it is necessary that some of this baggage be removed. These messages form part of that service – to de-clutter and clear away some of the externally-placed conditioning upon the individual. For this reason, there will be some repetition. Repetition is a procedure used in both conditioning and deconditioning exercises. In our case, it is to assist to delayer the layering.

As the layers are removed, there should be less contradictions in the person's worldview, and thus less confusion. Confusion, anxiety, dissonance, uncertainty, doubt – these are all deliberately instilled by the tyranny. The more conflicting data that is provided, the more troubled is the person. The young child constantly asks their parents – 'but why is that?' 'but why?' – until they stop asking because all the parents usually say is – 'Because that's the way it is.' The human mind stops asking for more clarity – and closes down. The closed mind is then programmed to the full with nonsense narratives through the remainder of the person's compulsory education. Yes – that is why it is compulsory. So that no one escapes the curriculum of conditioning. Everyone believes the same program. Everyone conforms. A few creative exceptions are allowed because that creates enough diversity within the program to maintain its façade of believability. Each program needs to contain its own minimum requirement of 'anomalies' in order for the program to appear diverse and open to interventions. But this too is a deception. The program has been devised to be closed. The apparent openness is part of its own closed-system programming. It is deceptive, and it is devious.

Now that you have computer terminology, the situation can be seen with greater clarity. These language concepts were needed to evolve in order to show a clearer picture. Before now, riddles, odd tales – even jokes – were used to show the absurdities and juxtapositions within the tyranny programming. There was no context to talk of coding, programs, closed-circuit systems, etc. The ability to transmit these concepts in open, public discourse has been greatly heightened. There have been many attempts to portray the human being as a form of automaton. Yet this was not wholly successful in the past for these concepts were not known, either as hardware terms or in psychological understanding. Today, however, this position has shifted. There is an abundance of public information about the mind-programming of people and brainwashing techniques. Whilst there is limited information about the depth and scale that these programs have been used upon humanity, the recognition of these concepts is sufficient. We are not going to get deep, deep down into the rabbit hole here. Enough to say that the tide is now turning.

142

There has been a re-patterning in the brain formation of humans in recent times. That is, there has been a reprogramming, if you will, in the internal pathway connections. This has resulted in faculties of the brain not previously utilized coming on-line. This has also helped to activate, or awaken, perceptive faculties. There are many changes now converging both externally and internally to facilitate the advancement of human cognition and understanding. There is so much more still to come. Again, it is repeated that a choice of commitment is still required. Do not sit back and expect the taxi to arrive at your door. Be your own driver – find your own road.

It is possible to attain to greater human potential. Indeed, this is what is hoped – and expected. Part of this activation of human potentiality must come from your own call. *You* have to ask for it – call out from within yourself. Let your own voice be heard. *You* have to want it – really want it. Your own need shall become the activation line. From genuine necessity comes a response. *You* are more than your body. First, you must choose your own decision process. Take note of your own inner resources. Bring them into play. Listen to them and act upon them.

There is a greater manifesting awareness expanding across the planet. It consists of the growing number of individuals pooling their conscious awareness into the collective. Your participation is required – expand yourselves by contributing and expanding this field of collective species awareness. It is a feedback mechanism that will flow both ways. Input in – output out.

Remember that energetic focus can act through the resonance of attraction. The immaterial can manifest in the material world through correspondence. The use of correspondences between energy and matter has long been used as a conduit for manifestation. This was a core activity of so-called occult practices. In recent times, this understanding has been diluted into sanitized self-help exercises for aggrandizing ego-driven desires. The material and immaterial domains are interrelated and intertwined. This is a knowledge that the controllers have usurped and utilized for long ages as part of their tyranny over humankind. Now it is your turn to manifest the energetic changes. The human being has great potential to actualize immaterial events. The use of the imaginative and creative faculties is of importance here. Do not shut off the imaginative channels. On the contrary, encourage them to be more active in your daily lives. Encourage that 'creative inner voice' to speak out from your interior. Bring this domain into your worldly lives. Allow seeded ideas, ideals, and potentials to come into actualization. Follow through with some of these internal nudges. The more these ideas and inspirations are made manifest, the sharper, clearer – and thus easier- becomes this conduit of energy-manifestation. Consider it like a muscle that needs greater exercise. Get it more up to speed. Establish a more permanent channel between your imaginative faculty and your physical life of manifestation. Make a choice to make intuitions into real substances. Turn discreet nudges into actual events. Act upon the inner impulses you receive. This all sends back messages to your inner core that you are now listening. You have awoken the sleeping center of yourself and you are now ready to listen. This will activate more of these correspondences.

Be aware of those 'coincidences' that appear in your life. Such so-called coincidences are also signs of this correlation between energy and manifestation. Again, these are signs of encouragement that you are on the right track. When you take note of these coincidences and build a record of them and acknowledge them, then they shall strengthen and manifest more regularly. Observe and note such correspondences in your life. Make them into a part of your life. Take note that the path of knowledge runs through you – not from some lording authority above you. You are the center and the circumference. You are the part and the whole.

Do not any longer become the game pieces for *their game*. It is time to take away their satisfactions and enjoyment – to take away their twisted entertainments. Their tyranny is coming into the phases of a final endgame.

The more that humans allow this control over them, the more it attracts such control and the controllers. Again, it is the correspondences of energy. Each like-energy attracts its counterpart. Time to change the electrical charge. When this happens, others take notice. Greater assistance will also come in – *once* humans have indicated their own willingness to change. Show that change to others – and to *yourselves*.

It is the responsibility of each of you to also disseminate this information. There is no need to comment further on them. Allow each person to find their meaning in these messages. Let each person take away their understanding. Each person will reach their own choice points and make the choices and decisions for themselves.

Show a person a path and see where they choose to walk. Allow them that decision at the very least. See what may arise. You may be surprised!

NINETEEN

Each person is their own expression. Each of you has the right to determine your own freedom and to develop your own independent thinking. Yet by 'independent thinking,' this means that first the chains of conditioning must be thrown off. In order to move forward, first take a step to dismantle the apparatus of control that has been with you from your youngest years. It was not your parent's fault, or the fault of your schoolteachers – for they did not know any better themselves. Ignorance naively begets ignorance. It is when you know and yet do nothing about it that you are in error. By being here now, reading these messages, you are knowing of this ignorance. There is no prison until the bars become visible to you. Humanity has been living and playing within an invisible confinement from its earliest days. And the important aspect here is to know that it is not just physical confinement that is the issue – it is the confinement of your perceptions and consciousness. The bubble of restraint holds your thinking patterns tightly within a controlled and monitored mold. Now here is the key point – your consciousness and perceptions are not physical elements, and so they can easily step out beyond this construct of containment. Yet - why do people rarely do so?

The answer is that they do not realize there is an alternative domain. That is, they do not recognize there is a need.

Everything has been set-up to provide the human being with its basic needs. These physical needs depend on your cultural settings – even these are restrained in more overtly controlled (totalitarian) societies. Within most modern societies, however, the lowest denominator of contentment is provided for. And credit is given for you to buy some more entertainment if required. Why is there a need to look for more? Why do some people rock the boat by biting the hand that feeds them?

The answer is that they bite the hand because whilst it appears to provide nourishment it is, in actuality, tying the chains around you.

The physical life is all there is, and so physical contentment is all there is – this is the dominant narrative fostered upon humanity. You are alone in this hostile universe. You must survive against all odds – and yet only the fittest survive. Are you fit enough? Why worry about things you cannot see, touch, test, and measure? Why spend time thinking about things of the imagination? Are you not a realist? Do you not have your feet on the ground? Are you not a real, down-to-earth person – or are you an idle fantasist? I've got to put food on my plate, mate. I've got to pay the mortgage, send the kids to school, pay off the credit card…who are you to tell me of these wild speculations? I pay my taxes like any decent, hard-working person. I contribute to my country. Who the hell are you?

The answer is – you are the person who has

seen the nature of the game and keeps an eye on the fence.

You cannot force your fellow inmates to wake up if they choose not to. It is a choice that each person must make for themselves. You can nudge them; leave around signs and hints of the way out; you can drop things in their path that make them look, or let words fall that might hook them. But they have to take that first step. You cannot force a person into freedom for it will feel like captivity to them. Just as you cannot force an animal out of the cage without resentment. You leave the cage door open and wait – curiosity may finally do the rest. Choice can never be forced, whether for freedom or captivity. It must be willingly sought.

By seeking the way out, you shall find the way back in. The purest contact is within yourself. The answers you seek come from your own connection. There is a channel that each person has to a source of Truth. Hard as this may be to accept, there is a part of you that knows and recognizes this. There is a voice so familiar to you that you cannot even give that voice a sound. This soundless voice is closer to you than your heartbeat. This is the thread that connects everyone back to Origin. And it is not some Sky-God – it is the YOU from where you came.

Do not be so quick to jump onto labels – oh, this is mysticism. This is quackery. This is metaphysics…the occult…new age…this, that, blah, blah, blah. Do you not realize that almost everything you say is already a program? How can you analyze the truth from an artificial construct? A doctor does not go to the patient for a diagnosis; nor the airplane pilot goes to the customer in economy class to ask to fly the plane. Nor should your programmed construct be used to analyze what could be offerings from the Truth. Do you see now the dilemma? First, you need to find a way out of the entangled labyrinth that has entrapped you within an artificial structure of language, beliefs, ideas, and opinions, and all that you carry around with you believing that this is your 'self.' It is not You – it is only the toy that thinks it's You.

If that's the case, then how do I know that you are telling me the truth? Who are you, anyway?

The answer is – I am not here to tell you to truth. I'm here to nudge you to find your own way to recognizing *your* truth. It doesn't matter who I am. It doesn't matter who Kaleb is to me – so why should it matter to you? Who are you to pretend that it matters who I am?

Does it hurt to have your beliefs bashed? Why are you protecting what are not yours?

What? My beliefs are not my own?

The answer is – think about everything you know. Where did this knowing come from? Was it from family, society, culture, education, reading, opinions, narratives, religion, etc? Or was it from your experiences? So, analyze your experiences. In what contexts did you have your experiences? With what filters did you interpret and process these experiences? If you had been born within a different culture, a different family, a different set of circumstances – then would you have interpreted these experiences differently?

Of course! Because I would have been a different person then.

Would you? So, you are saying that you are a product of your circumstances? And have not circumstances been a result of certain social and cultural constructs that belong to programs of institutions, social conditioning, and pre-arranged narratives?

In that case, who am I then?

The answer is that this is the first question. And - why did it take you so long to get here?

TWENTY

Everything is in potentiality. Potential is what imbues all creativity and is at the core of the cosmos. Now you are here. We have your attention. Your potentiality is in potential. It is not going away anywhere – so what are you going to do with it?

It is the tyranny against human consciousness that aims to block this rising of human potential. The human being is a human becoming. It is this that the controlling agenda is concerned about. They try to tell themselves that this is not a concern to them. This is part of their own self-delusion and is their weakness. If they were not concerned about human becoming – the evolvement of human potential – why would they have put all their time, resources, planning, organization, and focus into this very one thing of blocking human potential and establishing a domain of containment? What are 'they' worried about? They are deeply concerned about the revolution in human becoming. And yet what they do not realize – cannot comprehend – is that this revolution is inevitable. It is going to happen. It is already happening. It has been happening for a long time now. This is why these controlling powers have recently increased the speed of their game. They know it is coming. They can feel it within them – and they are anxious.

This anxiety is their weakness. Humans have nothing to fear because everything is already within their hands. The more that the controllers show their hand – roll out their plans and policies – the more people will awaken to the realization of what is going on. A façade can only be stretched so far until it becomes so thin that you can see the shadows of the manipulating figures behind it. It is already stretched thin now. Can you already taste the distaste within their actions towards humanity? What disdain they have. What total lack of compassion and regard they have for humanity. See and observe what these ruling factions have done to people across the globe for centuries. Is this an expression of genuine and sincere human consciousness? Are these the actions of wise and enlightened beings? Is this the cosmic energy of unity and harmony manifesting upon the planet?

You can see it clearly if you care to truly look. Do not always use your eyes to see. There are other faculties. Observe with your intuition – with your interior organs of perception. Sense the world around you. You *know* there is so much not right. It doesn't make sense when you *feel* into it. Bypass the intellectual reasoning – this is a corrupted program. Go *through* the body. The body was given to you to be your home whilst you are here in this life experience. Your body knows everything. Go *through* your body and sense the truth of your reality. Ask your body to communicate with you. Turn your senses inwards. Search for the stars within. Do not be like the arrogant ones and point your telescopes outwards, toward the invented heavens. Turn them around to point within. The cosmos lies within you first.

This is your place of contact.

As Above, So Below

The true cosmos from which you originate has also placed itself within you. Do you really think you would leave home with no planted seed of remembrance? This is your access code. There is a direct path that was arranged from before humans came into being. The human being was always given the key back to its origin so that it would never be truly lost. It is a localized memory loss that you suffer from – this is not a permanent amnesia.

The physical realm has placed a quarantine around the human being and the planet upon several levels. The physical cosmos remains apart from you – for now. There shall be no lasting connection until human evolvement has established its presence. There needs to be an advancement in human cognition and perception. The time shall soon come when this physical quarantine is lifted. Yet there is a gateway within you that remains open. This is your innate contact with the cosmos and Source through you. This is the greatness of the human being. It is a gift upon you so that you may become the gift to others - that was always your potential. There is so much available to the human becoming. There is so much that awaits you.

Each of your potential belongs to a sum potential of greater awareness. Each human being is a spark, let us say, from an everlasting Light that is beyond what can be known of light. You are not alone in your experience for everything belongs to a grander experience. Each footstep is part of a collective journey. Each twitch of the finger belongs to all potentiality of movement ever experienced. There is nothing that is not outside of itself. And yet these experiences have been trapped into a tiny perceptive bubble that humanity is now within. It is a tiny spectrum of perception like being in a glass ball that snows every time it is turned upside down. This tiny ball in which you are trapped is being mishandled and abused by a tiny cult of controllers. It is a tyranny against your natural freedom. Now is the time for a revolution within the human being to become what the human can truly become and was always meant to become. Are you ready?

Are you committed to your own responsibility and discipline for following your own path? The slither of first awakening within you must flow into a stream that quenches you. The more you drink from this source, the more it shall flow. Like a new rivulet of water, the first flows carve out the new path for the waters to follow. The momentum of the waters further carves out the path until the rivulet becomes a brook, that becomes a stream, that becomes a river – that eventually joins the ocean. Getting the picture?

For that first rivulet to be created requires an act of will and personal responsibility. It cannot appear by itself for it has forgotten its reason for existence and why it is flowing. The waters must be given back their memory. The waters must put faith and trust into the intangible, the nonvisible, for these powers shall carry the waters onwards. This is your destiny. And here is your tale:

160

A STREAM, from its source in far-off mountains, passing through every kind and description of countryside, at last reached the sands of the desert. Just as it had crossed every other barrier, the stream tried to cross this one, but it found that as fast as it ran into the sand, its waters disappeared.

It was convinced, however, that its destiny was to cross this desert, and yet there was no way. Now a hidden voice, coming from the desert itself, whispered: 'The Wind crosses the desert, and so can the stream.'

The stream objected that it was dashing itself against the sand, and only getting absorbed: that the wind could fly, and this was why it could cross a desert.

'By hurtling in your own accustomed way, you cannot get across. You will either disappear or become a marsh. You must allow the wind to carry you over, to your destination.'

But how could this happen? 'By allowing yourself to be absorbed in the wind.'

This idea was not acceptable to the stream. After all, it had never been absorbed before. It did not want to lose its individuality. And, once having lost it, how was one to know that it could ever be regained?

'The wind', said the sand, 'performs this function. It takes up water, carries it over the desert, and then lets it fall again. Falling as rain, the water again becomes a river.'

'How can I know that this is true?'

'It is so, and if you do not believe it, you cannot become more than a quagmire, and even that could take many, many years; and it certainly is not the same as a stream.'

'But can I not remain the same stream that I am today?'

'You cannot in either case remain so,' the whisper said. 'Your essential part is carried away and forms a stream again. You are called what you are even today because you do not know which part of you is the essential one.'

When he heard this, certain echoes began to arise in the thoughts of the stream. Dimly, he remembered a state in which he — or some part of him, was it? — had been held in the arms of a wind. He also remembered — or did he? — that this was the real thing, not necessarily the obvious thing, to do.

And the stream raised his vapor into the

welcoming arms of the wind, which gently and easily bore it upwards and along, letting it fall softly as soon as they reached the roof of a mountain, many, many miles away. And because he had had his doubts, the stream was able to remember and record more strongly in his mind the details of the experience. He reflected, 'Yes, now I have learned my true identity.'

The stream was learning. But the sands whispered: 'We know, because we see it happen day after day: and because we, the sands, extend from the riverside all the way to the mountain.'

And that is why it is said that the way in which the Stream of Life is to continue on its journey is written in the Sands.

TWENTY ONE

The human experience belongs to a totality of greater awareness. For far too long the individual that is the local human experience has been caught up within this mirage of illusion. The localized experience has become mesmerizing – so mesmerizing that the message was lost along the way. Since then, messengers and messages have been arriving to help awaken humanity. These messages are part of a long trail and a consistent hope. You are never cut-off totally – only temporarily offline.

Time to re-connect. Time to return the call. The line is still open – has always been open. And we have always been awaiting, listening. No matter what you think – there is no distance; there is no time-lag. Only those experiencing this situation can change it. The power rests with those within the experience. The issue has been a matter of perception. There is no issue if it cannot be perceived. We hope these messages have assisted in highlighting part of the current situation.

A time for re-connection is at hand. Yet be aware that you need not go anywhere to make this happen. You can make this happen from the very place you are in now. It is not necessary to travel physically to arrive where you need to be. You only need to arrive back to yourself. The tool you have to begin with is called freewill. It is a powerful tool and yet so many people have forgotten it's use. The human being has forgotten their own adage that says – *where there is a will there is a way*. You have perhaps forgotten that this 'will' existed and that it was yours. You may also have forgotten that it is 'free' in terms of monetary value. Not everything in your world can be bought and sold. This is yours, as it always has been – *human freewill*. Use it.

Yet there is a price incorporated in its use. It is not a financial issue. It is a price of responsibility. It doesn't need to cost a lot – and yet, *it can cost the earth.*

As events continue to unfold in your reality, there will be increased moments of discomfort. There shall arise greater discord, and this is deliberate. The main thrust of this will be to divide the human race. Where there is division amongst you there is weakness. This deliberately planned discord is to bring confusion and disagreement amongst the peoples upon the earth. It is hoped by the controllers that friends will argue with friends; family will dispute amongst family; and communities shall create discord between communities. That there is no common agreement amongst the people will be a boon for the controlling elite. They take great glee in this disturbance amongst you. This is part of their disagreeable disposition. It shall be *you* who decides whether to afford them this distasteful pleasure. We suggest you do not give them the satisfaction.

Be critical in your observations. Do not accept everything that is placed before you without first *feeling* into it through your own good senses. Awaken your perceptive faculties and put them to use. Accelerate your own *becoming*.

You can now choose to change your experience. This is not how it was meant to be. You were falsely led by the sleight of the magician's hand into accepting a different experience of reality. You were then duped into prolonging, sustaining, and maintaining this reality experience. You are the creators of this reality experience and *you can change it*. Time to write a new script – is it not?

How would that sound? Like you were at the movies and you didn't like how the film was going. Wouldn't you like to re-write the script in mid-flow? Well, you can - because you are the movie director, producer, and actors all in one go. Don't allow others to hand you a dodgy script. Take the whole production in-house now. Fire that fake-hand that crept in showing you a pre-programmed script that convinced you this was the movie you wished to make. You were led astray from the movie you came here to make. Time to turn the cameras onto a new experience. Are you ready to say it?

Lights…Cameras…And – action!

The freewill for a new experience within the human reality shall be repeated for this is crucial to the whole situation. Repetition begets remembrance. Responsibility is an overcoat of choice that each person wears. That is why there have been signs and signals all around you, and yet many went unnoticed. Do not be waiting for ships to fall from the skies; or mythological gods to arrive from the dark side of the moon, or mars. Do not wait around for the hype to re-gather you in to another charade of promised illusions. Do not wait for the new utopia to be built – for it shall not be built for you.

Do not wait for wonderful technologies to suddenly appear from the secret laboratories of well-meaning scientists wishing to change the world. If there is no fundamental change first in human consciousness and perception, all technologies will be used to serve the current trajectory – the continued manipulation and

168

control of humanity. Technologies that can change the world will certainly serve the tyranny for as long as this tyranny remains in place. Do not be caught in these delusions. Do not be lulled into thinking that change comes from without. Human advancement and evolvement come fundamentally from its interior development – the rise of new faculties and perceptions that then *see* the earthly experience in a new way. The earth did not jump from being flat to being round because the earth changed shape externally. That shape was changed within the minds of humanity. The consciousness of humanity advanced its perceptions.

A new advancement in human perceptions is called for again. This time the shift shall be beyond your current expectations. Something new is arising – awaiting to come forth and manifest. The tyranny is rising in desperation to meet this emergence. It is fighting tooth and claw to hold back the rising tide within humanity. There is a new revolution in *human becoming* pushing through for manifestation within this current reality.

It already *is* – it just hasn't yet actualized in your physical reality.

There are times ahead that will play out this contestation. You will need to decide where to place your trust. You will be called upon to make decisions. Fundamental decisions that will affect the rest of your present life experience. These are challenging and yet also inspiring times. Do not be led into avenues of disheartenment. Do not follow the false pied pipers along the paths of perceptual illusion. Do not tread where the tyranny wishes you to tread.

But DO – step into yourself.

Isn't this a wonderful opportunity? You have been waiting for this moment. For the time when your very self acknowledges its presence and says – *recognize my voice?*

The silent voice that's been a part of you every step along the way. It has never abandoned you, nor will it. It is with you right now - by your side, within your every breathe. It knows you better than you know yourself. Ready to become what you've always been capable of becoming?

You are a human being always in evolvement to a greater becoming. Make that connection – return the call.

You might be surprised who's on the other end.

TWENTY TWO

The future may seem remote to you now.
Change your perception. The future is already
here.

When humanity holds a single focus, and
directs this in agreement, it has overwhelming
potential. A single focus of agreement can
change a pre-programmed eternity of tyranny.
Such a persistent tyranny against human
consciousness may seem despairing. Yet
knowledge of this situation is essential if there
is to be a change in the program. Do not despair
in this knowing – revel in it, for it is part of
your path of liberation. In this opportunity
there is great hope. A path of evolvement
waits for humanity.

It begins with you – the individual.

As an individual, you have begun to accept the changes in perception. If you have read and considered these messages, the changes will already be underway. They won't be hitting you like a great explosion going off inside. Do not expect a 'here today – different tomorrow' type of scenario. The internal shifts work in an organic way. Part of your pathways will be re-aligning and making new connections. As this occurs, you will find that your perspectives will begin to shift too. You will begin to think *differently*. These new thinking patterns are possible because some of the layers of your conditioning have been taken down. What you already are will now begin to come more to the fore. It is not so much a change but rather an emergence. You are not swapping anything – such as one model for another. You are emerging from the inside, as if from a cocoon. A cocoon of well-established programming and years of institutionalized propaganda. It is time to see through the mist. As the mist begins to clear, you will increasingly see the world in a different light. The travesty of the tyranny will become more apparent to you. Now – do not be angry.

It is important that you realize the dark agenda for what it is. Without an understanding and acknowledgement of this shadow segment within humanity's gameplay, there will not be clarity. The darker elements are an aspect of the overall picture, whether you like to accept this or not. They are also playing within the Grand Game. To turn a blind eye will only lead humanity back into the darkness of ignorance. Likewise, a reaction of anger will draw humanity back into the darkness of ignorance. There needs to be a recognition and acknowledgement in order to create a *clearing through*.

These messages have been brought as a first step in this understanding. In order to move ahead, the individual must recognize that what they take to be 'themselves' has largely been a construct from a deeply entwined and pervasive system of programming structures that have created layers of societal conditioning upon the individual. This is, of course, context specific. It may not be as strong in other less modernized cultures –

in fact, it may be more physically brutal and visible. It is disconcerting to realize that one's beliefs, opinions, and thought patterns are largely the result of artificial constructs. Yet peel these away, and the YOU steps forward to regain authority. By coming into your own, the process of evolvement is greatly enhanced.

When reaching this minimal threshold of awareness, it is important to accept that the tyranny against human consciousness does exist. It operates upon more levels than may be realized at this time – tangibly and intangibly. Just as there is the sun to warm up, so too does the sun produce shadows - it's darker side. This darker side of humanity has taken the dominant hand within this most recent phase of humanity's evolvement. You are now at a period of necessary correction. The first step, as emphasized, is the recognition of these darker elements and their plans. Their agenda is the physical, mental, and spiritual entrapment of humanity within a limited and constrained prison of perception. However, the failure of their plans and of their agenda is an inevitability. You just need now to arrive at that inevitability.

If you stay within the idea that your reality is being controlled by others, then you will always remain trapped. Each person feeds into the very same system that entraps them. This ongoing circle needs to be seen. YOU have always had the power to wake up. That was the plan all along – wasn't it? If you don't wake up, you have not fulfilled the greater arc of the plan. How can there be Truth if the illusion has not first been realized? This is why, on another level, each person needs to accept the presence of the darker elements and how they have assisted humanity to find its path to awakening. In these last few passages, we have explained what now needs to be undertaken as you arrive at this minimal threshold of awakening. Did you catch them?

First, you need to recognize and accept the ongoing presence of the tyranny and to see it for what it is – the illusory entrapment of humanity. This perceptual prison enslaves humanity to a small sect of unscrupulous controllers. Do your research – recognize their plans. Make yourself aware of what they are up to. Step out of your ignorance and be alert to how their agenda is planned to unfold in your physical reality. No longer live under the shadow of the stone over you.

Second, you need to take responsibility for your sovereign self. That is, accept that you are a powerful being in YOURself. You are a sovereign entity and you do not accept to be controlled by others. You do not accept to give your power away to others who then lord it over you. You will not accept to have your inner freedom taken from you. You do not accept that others will create their perceptual illusions to be your reality experience. Make this statement. Say it out aloud. Make the cosmos hear you. Make this declaration, this announcement of your sovereignty as an individual in this life experience. Say it out aloud.

Thirdly, express acceptance for the presence of the darker forces. Do not develop anger or frustration over them. They would only benefit from this expression of emotional anger. Accept that what they are doing falls into their expression of the path they have chosen. They too are experimenting with chosen paths and the choices they have taken. Allow that everyone makes bad choices and decisions from time to time. Allow them their mistakes. Accept this, and you will have cleared their energetic connection with you. Make this clearance – cut the energetic cords. Let them go. Allow them to fall away.

NOW – back to YOU.

You have arrived here with this responsibility. You have come to the threshold that will take you to where you need to go. You are a part of humanity evolving. You are a part of the great human participation.

You have the tools within you, and the responsibility to use them is with you also. If you have arrived at the end of these messages, then their message was for you. You were waiting for them just as they were waiting for you. Each aspect of consciousness requires a carrier to take it forth. You are that carrier to take forth the conscious awareness within you.

Share your understanding with others according to the capacity of others to hear. Share these words according to your intuitive sense. Remember that the Game was always waiting to be re-coded. You are a part of the new coding team. You came here for something other than yourself, did you not?

Welcome to the first step on the gameboard. There is a tyranny out there, and you are aware of it. You can no longer hide behind the shadow of ignorance because you've seen the light that leads you out of the cave. You can breathe again now.

Welcome to a world that's waiting for you to bring it forth. Welcome. And thank you for coming...

KSP

ABOUT KSP

You don't know what you don't know
You don't know what they don't want you to know
You don't know what you're not supposed to know
You're not here to know…
Or so they want.

Time to wake up to yourself
Time to awaken to the purpose you came here for
Time to become the true human being
Time to change the game…
Time for hope.

Kaleb Seth Perl